THE STAGE IN ACTION

THE STAGE IN ACTION

THE PLAYERS

Alert, controlled, ready. Two figures in Arnold Sundgaard and Marc Connelly's *Everywhere I Roam*, produced by Marc Connelly and Bela Blau.

THE
STAGE
IN ACTION

BY SAMUEL SELDEN
University of North Carolina

Illustrated by Wautell Selden

F. S. CROFTS & CO.
New York   *1946*

PREFACE

The first title selected for this book was *Design in the Dramatic Performance*. Several experienced people to whom the name was submitted replied that it was misleading. The word "design," as applied to the theatre, they declared, connotes one thing only, the visual background. "Stage design" is the art of planning scenery, lighting, and costumes—the *environment* of action, not the action itself.

The critics were right, of course. That their answer should have admitted no argument is regrettable. Apparently without any protest, the actors and directors in this country have allowed their technical colleagues to usurp for their exclusive use a word which should be applicable to every creative department of the theatre. Design is defined by the dictionary as "the arrangement of details which make up a work of art." We speak of the design of a poem, of a novel, of a piece of sculpture, of a building. With reference to the stage, we speak of the design of a setting, properties, costumes, lighting. Yet, when we refer to the sensitive and logical arrangement of vocal and pantomimic action into an effective dramatic performance, we hesitate to use the term "design." Why?

The reason lies doubtless in the fact that today most

v

American directors and actors still labor to be "natural," and one does not characterize a "natural" product as "designed." Long ago the shrewder technical artists learned that too much preoccupation with simple imitation dulls the effect of a work of art. Many of the leading scenic men were originally easel painters, and from their experience outside the theatre they brought the knowledge that common, everyday shapes—walls, doorways, trees, and even tables and chairs—if they are to speak eloquently to the human eye, must be adapted, within themselves and especially in their relationship with one another. There must be selection, and certain features must be changed, exaggerated, idealized, and arranged for interest and stimulation. In other words, the objects must be *designed*.

Since early in the present century the scenic artists have been helped in their work by lighting engineers. Improvements in the control and adjustment of stage lighting have made possible more varieties of stage atmosphere. In more recent years the musical composers have increased the scope of tonal utterance. A number of leading playwrights in this country and Europe have taken advantage of the scenic and musical means now at their disposal to produce new play forms. They, like the scenic artists and musicians, are aware of the importance of looking beyond realism and of searching for fresh effects through experimental design.

The two groups of dramatic artists who seem most consistently to have lagged behind in the progress toward a more genuinely dynamic and richly emotional theatre are, first, the actors, and, second (only to a slightly lesser degree), the directors. Whenever the members of these two groups are reproached for their lack of courage in experimental effort, they usually reply that they wish to remain "true to life." But too often they cannot state clearly just what they mean by that truth. The amateur with a camera who, on a Sunday afternoon stroll, "snaps" a view across the hills produces a picture which is in one sense faithful to the landscape. But the artist who comes to the same hills may paint an interpretation which, though it departs in certain details from the forms observed, is essentially much truer to the character of the landscape than the precise record in the photograph.

Because the art of representing men and women on the stage is necessarily mimetic, acting can never employ abstractive methods—selection, exaggeration, distortion, re-ordering—to the same degree as painting. The material to be translated is human behavior. The stage media are fixed and direct: human bodies and human voices. Consequently, the dramatic artist who insists that his means of expression are different from those in other fields argues with some logic. But the artist in the theatre, like the one outside, who doggedly insists on "naturalness" to the exclusion of everything else achieves in the end sterility. Many of those young actors and directors who loudly proclaim their adherence to the doctrine of "truth to living" lose all sense of the objective values in their work and retire aggressively into a narrowly subjective technique which they mistakenly feel to be reality. Superficially following the advice of a Stanislavsky to go back to nature, and profoundly misunderstanding the way in which that great teacher viewed and *managed* nature, they spend their efforts in trying to stand on solid earth, but never learn to leap and run.

It has long been my conviction that these people of the stage would enrich their work immeasurably if they viewed it through the eyes of other artists, and if they brought consciously to the service of their acting and directing certain fundamental principles which have proved their worth in other fields. The purpose of this book is to provide a broader understanding of the problems involved in effective dramatic performance by looking at them from a fresh viewpoint. Special attention is directed to the practical relationships between acting and directing and two other creative forms: dancing and music. In connection with directing, some comparisons are also made with the graphic arts.

No creative effort has any really functional foundation, of course, unless it drives its roots deep into the soil of human living. The theatre has suffered from too many theories which—ingenious as they may be—are based upon nothing deeper than the immediate problems of technique. In an attempt to keep the present discussion on a sound footing, I have based it upon the demands of the theatre audience, and have devoted the first chapter to the playgoer. The entire discussion is based, ultimately, upon the aesthetic needs of this audience. The second chapter deals with the magic forces of rhythm and tone, and the third and fourth chapters take up, step by step, the practical relationships between the techniques of dancer and pantomimist and of singer and speaker. Chapter Five explores the meaning of action; and the next three divisions are concerned with the synthesis of all the different lively elements of a stage production into a single pictorial unity. The final chapter returns the attention of the dramatic designer to the audience and its peculiar habits of response to the designer's work.

Throughout, the problems of the actor and the director are considered together, because they are essentially one. The technique of the director in staging a performance involving several actors simply extends a little the primary technique of the individual actor. The function of the director is to see the actor's performance in perspective. He concerns himself, more than the player in the thick of action can, with the broad sweep of the performance as a whole, the effective association of all the different dramatic elements. But fundamentally the director's problems of movement and sound are the same as the actor's.

The examples used in the text are drawn, partly from the theatre, partly, as we have already intimated, from the other arts. Many of the illustrations are taken from the experiences of everyday life. The reader will doubtless notice that in the stage examples some partiality is shown toward the plays of one author, Mr. Paul Green. There are two reasons why his name occurs frequently in the following pages. One is that I have had the privilege of directing eight of his plays and feel consequently that I possess with respect to the staging of them a more practical working knowledge than I have with most other authors' compositions. The second reason is that I feel that this author's works lend themselves more naturally than do those of any other modern playwright to the discussion of dramatic dance and song.

I wish to express my warm gratitude to the John Simon Guggenheim Memorial Foundation, whose generosity opened the way for the preparation of this book. Many friends, in and out of the theatre, helped in its making. I regret that I cannot mention all of them here. I can, however, state my special indebtedness to Ruth Hadfield Smith, whose patient and efficient editorial assistance in a busy season made the construction of the manuscript possible. I wish to extend my thanks to the *Theatre Arts Monthly*, the Museum of Modern Art, the Macbeth and E. Weyhe galleries, and to Benton Spruance, Betty Joiner, and Polly Perkins for permission to reproduce several drawings and paintings. Also, I wish to thank the photographers for their kindness in allowing me to use their prints.

Samuel Selden

CONTENTS

Chapter Nine

THE RESPONSE OF THE AUDIENCE

HALFTONE ILLUSTRATIONS

THE STAGE IN ACTION

THE STAGE IN ACTION

Chapter One

THE AUDIENCE
AND THE ACTOR

WHY DO PEOPLE
GO TO THE THEATRE?

Mrs. Morley rinses and dries the last of her supper dishes, spreads the towel on the rod by the stove, and hangs up her apron, as she has done countless times before. She sits for a moment to rest; then she rises and crosses the hall to have a look at the window shade about which the new lodger has complained. Having adjusted it—Mr. Brown could so easily have fixed it himself!—she sighs. Today has been particularly trying.

Suddenly she remembers: at the Auditorium tonight a touring company is giving a play called *You Can't Take It with You.* Swiftly she slips into her coat. Soon she is standing in front of the theatre box office, and four minutes later she is seated in the balcony waiting for the curtain to rise. Beside her, in the same row, are Miss Farrand, assistant in the town library; Mr. Peters, proprietor of a small radio shop; Miss Johns, a salesgirl

1

from a department store; and Professor Smith from the neighboring college.

Why are they here? For what reason are these five people, and the seven hundred other people just like them, in the theatre tonight? If one could ask that question of every person present, he would doubtless receive a wide variety of answers, answers reflecting many different temperaments in many kinds of circumstances. But if one could secure all those answers, shake them down and sift them, he would draw three simple, basic conclusions. And these conclusions would explain the attendance at the Auditorium not only tonight, but every night a play—or film—is given there.

The first conclusion would be that people come to a theatre for *diversion*.* They desire a change. They wish to forget for a little while the experiences of the day by having their minds carried to new faces and different adventures. The second conclusion would be that people come for *stimulation*. In the theatre their emotions are exercised. Every person, even the most sophisticated, needs to laugh and cry occasionally, to feel passionately about something; to have his sense of expectation sharpened, and his affections, deadened by frustration or mere routine, awakened again to tenderness. The third desire— not of everyone, perhaps, but of such people as Miss Farrand, Professor Smith and many like them—is *clarification*. Keenly anticipated by thoughtful playgoers are the interpretive comments on human life made by the author and performer, sometimes seriously but often hu-

---

* These conclusions are based on answers to an actual questionnaire presented to three different theatre audiences.

THE AUDIENCE

A glimpse of the spectators at a performance of *Aaron Slick from Punkin Crick*, "greatest of all rural comedies," by Lieut. Beale Cormack.

THE AUDIENCE

Children watching a marionette show on Boston Common.

morously, in and between the lines of the play. Especially in our present period of political, economic, and moral confusion, serious people everywhere are looking for truth in thinking, and they turn to the dramatic philosophers for aid in their search. The best of the stage compositions have an illuminating value, help the spectator to see himself, other men, and the world at large more understandingly. And they go further, for when they both clarify and stimulate, these plays inspire new vision, exaltation, and purpose.

The desires for diversion, stimulation, and clarification find their most intensive satisfaction in the theatre. That is why more people are drawn there night after night than to any other institution in the world. In the playhouse, those primary human wishes are fulfilled through the magic means of *character*, *story*, and *comment*. These three elements constitute the fundamental substances of a dramatic performance.

But any reference to them alone fails to indicate the whole fascination of the theatre, to explain finally how those first three desires of the spectator are met. One thing more must be added to character, story, and comment; that is *the way in which they are presented*.

THE MANNER
OF THE PERFORMANCE

The way, or manner, of a presentation varies greatly from play to play because it is necessarily dependent on the kind of character, story, and comment which it projects. Founded on the idea of mirroring as closely as possible a certain kind of human behavior for a play like Elmer Rice's *Street Scene* or Sidney Kingsley's *Dead End,* or planned in accordance with a freer design for a play like Strindberg's *The Spook Sonata* or Kaiser's *Gas,* the dramatic mode may range all the way from realism to abstraction. Whether the purpose of the play is "expressionistic," "impressionistic," "romantic," "classical," or purely "naturalistic," the mode establishes it. Mode performs, therefore, a central part in the creation of dramatic effect.

ANCIENT DANCE
Figures from a Greek vase.

The behavior of the actors on a stage can never be given, of course, exactly like that of their prototypes in everyday life. That is obvious. Even in the performances of such "slice-of-life" plays as Kingsley's *Dead End,* the patterns of movement and speech have to be ordered for the theatre. There has to be a certain simplification and amplification to make the characters clear and poignant; a certain pointing to give the story direction; a certain sense of underlining to make the playwright's comment stand out. If the actors took no thought for the manner of their speech and pantomime, but huddled and mumbled as people do in everyday life, the character, story, and philosophy of a play would soon be lost to an audience. Effective mode makes the play "come over" the footlights. However, there is a reason much deeper than this one why considerations of dramatic mode occupy such a central position in the theatre.

REALISM AND ABSTRACTION IN ACTING

It is often fascinating to see on the stage certain familiar aspects of human behavior, as it were, in a mirror. The spectator may catch in the gestures and words of the players human details which are so like those seen in the people with whom he has long been acquainted that he gasps with delight at the miracle of transcription. Watching the lifelike movements and intonations of the players on the stage, and the very real setting behind them, the spectator derives the same type of pleasure as when he views a landscape, a portrait, or a still-life painting, which is "just like" a scene, a person, or objects, he knows.

But there is another pleasure which the spectator draws out of action which is moved at least one degree from realism. This is not action contrary to human behavior but action which represents the essences of this behavior. It is action which is free, rhythmical, and so controlled that it emphasizes and directs attention with telling effect. This is action touched by abstraction. The delight the spectator takes in following pantomime and speech "abstracted" out of the real toward the ideal is the pleasure one has from all stimulating, heightened effects. The element of abstraction helps to excite the perceptual faculties of the spectator, and, by these means, to stir up an emotional attitude toward the objects on the stage.

THE DRAMATIC
DANCE AND SONG

The two great factors for abstraction in the mode of a performance are *dance* and *song*. Every actor and every director working for potent effects in the theatre must know how to use these factors expertly, for on the use of *dance* and *song* depends the sense of *poetry* in the theatre.

Dance and song are not new elements of drama; they have always existed. But only in recent years has the real force of their values been rediscovered. This is shown in the growing number of verse plays and plays using choreography and music as an integral part of the performance. How fundamental are dance and song is evident as soon as one considers the origin of dramatic art, and, farther back than that, the origin of all the time arts—notably music and poetry.

Every form of vocal and instrumental music we hear

today is descended, we are told, from the primitive song and dance. In the beginning there were simple grunts and cries, inarticulate expressions of joy in the hunt or battle, or grief over the loss of a comrade, perhaps a mother moaning by the body of a child. Little by little the grunts and cries became connected and extended and were elaborated into tonal chants, sounded first by a single person, and later by a whole company of huntsmen, warriors, or mourners. In time, out of these crude sound forms of the savage, came the early folk songs, then the art songs and other types of music.

COMIC DANCER
From a Greek vase.

Coincident with the birth and development of song was the dance; first, probably, just a few formless movements, the leaping of a happy hunter, the prancing of a young lover, or the swaying back and forth of mourners. Gradually, as the ecstasy of passion possessed the savage, the convulsive swaying and leaping movements took on more and more rhythmic shape, and a dance was created. Soon it became a communal thing, entered upon deliberately by a company of persons desirous of expressing some common emotion, in a form which could be repeated whenever occasion demanded—before battle, at mating time, when the gods had to be propitiated for the harvest. And so, in time, there developed the various folk dances of the world; and these contributed to music the important element of meter.

Until instruments came into wide use in the seventeenth century, dance had less influence on musical structure than did song. With the composition of the suite and the sonata, however, dance and song became indissolubly blended.[1] The presence of the two elements is nowhere more evident now than in the great symphonic form. There one can recognize readily the solo, duet, quartet, and choral effects derived from singing. The four sections of the orchestra which renders this music are still referred to as "voices" or "choirs." Nearly all the great composers have received inspiration from simple vocal forms, and some of them have incorporated folk songs bodily into the tonal structure of their works. Dvořák's New World Symphony is a conspicuous example. While one senses in the sonorous forms of this instrumental music the presence of song, one senses in the metrical forms the presence of dance. In fact, the early symphonies developed out of dance suites; and a dance term (*minuet*, later *scherzo*) continues to be associated with the third movement. "Indeed," remarks one critic, "a dance still lingers always at the heart of music and even at the heart of the composer. Mozart, who was himself an accomplished dancer, used often to say, so his wife stated, that it was dancing, not music, that he really cared for. Wagner believed that Beethoven's Seventh Symphony—to some of us the most fascinating of them [the symphonies] and the most purely musical—was an apotheosis of the dance, and, even if that belief throws no light on the intention of Beethoven, it is at least a revelation of Wagner's own feeling for the dance."[2]

What has been said regarding the origin and development of music can be said with equal truth about verse. Poetry doubtless started as semiformless chanting, closely akin to early singing. There was the same striving for lyrical expression in changing tonal patterns. But there was no true rhythmic design until the speaker began to stride back and forth and stamp his feet for emphasis at certain

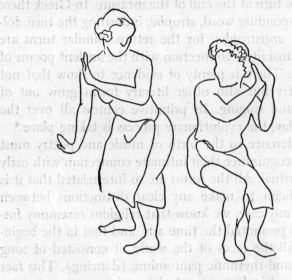

PRIMITIVE CEREMONIAL DANCE

points in the utterance. Max Müller, the German philologist, points out: "In Greek, *chorus* means dance, measured movement, and the Greek choruses were originally dances; nay, it can be proved that these dancing movements formed really the first metres of true poetry. Language itself bears witness to the fact that the oldest metres were the steps and movements of dancers. As the old dances consisted of steps, the ancient metres consisted of feet. Even we ourselves still speak of feet, not because we understand what it means, but simply because the Greeks and Romans spoke of feet, and they said so because originally the feet really marked the metre." [3] Our word "verse" is also a dance term, coming from the Latin *versus*, the turn at the end of the measure. In Greek there is a corresponding word, *strophe*, indicating the turn, followed by *antistrophe*, for the return. Similar turns are used in Sanskrit in connection with the ancient poems of the Veda. There is plenty of evidence to show that not only poetry but also other literary forms grow out of dancing and singing. In primitive centers all over the world today, the evolutionary process is taking place. [4]

Any reference to the birth of music and poetry must take into cognizance their intimate connection with early religious ritual. All the forms are so interrelated that it is often difficult to make any clear distinctions between them. In any case, we know that religious ceremony fostered and promoted the time arts, and that in the beginning, in all the races of the world, it consisted of song chanting and rhythmic pantomime (dancing). This fact may be read in history and observed in every primitive community today. In the exercises and services of even the more advanced religions, traces of dance and song are clearly discernible. King David composed and sang psalms addressed to God. It is also recorded that he danced before the Lord with all his might. So danced the prophets. So did Miriam and other persons mentioned in the Bible. There is evidence also that the first Christians expressed their reverent love for their Savior physically as well as vocally. Some writers have even argued that the Christian church was originally a theatre, the "choir" being a raised stage enclosed for dancing.[5] There was dancing in English cathedrals until the fourteenth century. In various churches of France it continued up to the seventeenth century, in Roussillon up to the eighteenth. On certain

EARLY FOLK DANCE

holy days there were dances before the high altar of the Cathedral of Seville as late as 1914. On some festival days in Mexico, joyous dancing is still practiced in the churches.

If music, poetry, and religious ceremony trace their double origin to the tonal and saltatory urges of primitive people, then drama, which developed from these three forms of activity, must admit the same origin. As far as our western theatre is concerned, we have direct evidence

of this ancestry. Attic drama, which is generally conceded
to be one of the two principal forebears of our own, sprang
out of the *dithyramb* and the *choros*, the first a religious
hymn in honor of Dionysos, and the second a group
dance, also religious. The ritualistic church drama of the
pre-Renaissance period, second forebear of our modern
theatre forms, was composed in verse and chanted to
music. Though here the forms are not directly dance and
song, they bear the mark of their descent from these.
Mystery, miracle, and later the morality plays were designed in tonal-rhythmical patterns, and so the tradition
of a pulsative, essentially musical dialogue and pantomime continued.

Renaissance drama, flowering in England in the work
of Shakespeare and his contemporaries, was, like the
classical and medieval, a verse drama. The actors' rendering of it was, therefore, bound to be to some extent songlike and dancelike. As long as poetry held the theatre
(from the sixteenth to the nineteenth century), the vocal
delivery of the performers was marked by a tonal play, and
their pantomime by a measured swing, which clearly
manifested their origins. It is true that in time much of
the intoning and gesturing became stiff and affected, but
even in their corrupted state they carried the stamp of
song and dance.

During the eighteenth century, many of the plays of
western Europe adopted a frankly operatic style. At the
close of the nineteenth century, the forms of dancelike
and songlike expression had become so thoroughly artificial, divorced from the content of the plays for which
they served as media, that there had to be a change. The

reformers raised a cry (echoes of which we are still hearing today), "Back to Nature!" Altering the design of the written play, removing every trace of sham in word and movement, working always for "realistic" effect, they threw verse out the window and denied any place in the

CHILD OF SIXTEENTH CENTURY SINGING
After an old print.

actor's performance to dance and song. In trying to clear out *dead* forms of dialogue and gesture, the extremists cleared out *all* forms.

But poets and artists cannot long suppress their lyrical and rhythmical impulses. And audiences soon grow tired of performances given without some sense of idealization —the selection, ordering, and heightening of tonal and pantomimic effects for the most eloquent expression. Consequently, in the work of the leading authors, actors, directors, and scenic designers, we find again today the fundamental factors of dancing and singing. Often they are very subtly disguised under the cloak of "realism," but they are there.

Chapter Two

MAGIC IN RHYTHM AND TONE

DANCING AND SINGING
ARE INHERENTLY STIMULATING

Our investigation of the relationship between the audience and the actor has led us to one general conclusion: the player fulfills his function most effectively when he performs, not like the everyday man in the workaday world, but as a doer and speaker moved by rhythm and music. The essential factors of dancing and singing, we say, give to the art of acting basic dramatic values.

Just what are these values? The fundamental answer is a simple one. Dancing and singing are inherently stimulating. They activate the human organism. Consequently, the values which they contribute to acting are dynamic. Dance and song make a performance *move*.

15

THE INFLUENCE OF DANCING

Dancing increases the pulse beat, stimulates the whole body, exhilarates the mind, lifts man away from the burden of gravity, and gives him a joyous sense of freedom and power. Under the spell of rhythmical movement, men perform superhuman deeds. Savages whip themselves into a frenzy and go forth to battle heedless of fear and pain. Primitive priests in their rituals leap high into the air, and do feats of extraordinary strength and endurance. Young German mountain climbers, swinging rhythmically up the faces of rocks in a kind of hypnotic dance, scale cliffs which are utterly impassable under any other technique.

It has been observed that the psychophysiological effects of dancing are similar to the psychophysiological results of drinking. Many dancers at a ball reach, without liquor, an intoxication similar to that caused by champagne or whisky. Prolonged and intensive movement produces a state of ecstasy. A. E. Crawley, in an article on dancing in the *Encyclopaedia of Religion and Ethics*, states that the dance with its power of producing tumescence was the original form of the orgy.[1]

Dancing exhilarates the whole human organism, and produces a state of trancelike excitement. The Bororo medicine men, by dancing and singing for several hours, work themselves into a state of hypnotic madness. The dancing dervish cuts himself with knives and eats live coals. Russian sectaries inflict upon themselves great wounds, unaware of pain. Travelers in the South Sea islands and elsewhere tell of the extraordinary effects of pulsative movement on all childlike people. Their muscles tremble from head to foot, even their jaws trembling, without any apparent ability on their part to control the shaking. They gesticulate like lunatics; their bodies jerk as though in convulsions; only the whites of their eyes show, while strange, wild, animal-like noises come from their throats. Sometimes they foam at the mouth and end their movements by falling in a paroxysm on the ground. That rhythmical, saltatory action may lift a man from all worldly ties to a feeling of transport is attested by those who have gone joyfully to their death while dancing. Savage chieftains, condemned to the gallows, have been known to dance to the scene of their execution. African pygmies, passionately preoccupied by their own movements and oblivious to everything around them, allowed themselves in the Boer War to be surrounded and shot down in droves while dancing. There is a report that once, fleeing from Turkish soldiers, sixty Greek girls, mothers, and children danced the old *romaiika* as they threw themselves one after another over a precipice.[2]

"Every dance is and gives ecstasy," says Curt Sachs in *World History of the Dance.* "The adult who puts his arm around his companion in the ball room, and the child in the roadway, skipping in a round dance—they forget themselves, they dissolve the weight of earthly contact and the rigidity of daily existence."[3] They enter the realm of spirit. Nothing indicates more clearly the hypnotic exhilaration enjoyed by the dancer than his almost inconceivable staying powers in a state of high tension. John Lawson, describing the Indians of North Carolina, reports

that they would "dance for several nights together with
the greatest briskness imaginable, their wind never failing
them." [4] Sachs tells of similar feats of endurance in
other tribes. For a dance to be continued through a whole
night is normal. "At her first period of menstruation a
girl of the California Achomawi dances for ten full nights,
and among the Guaicurú in the Gran Chaco a suitor must
dance 'convulsively' for eight days in front of the house
of his maiden." [5] We have present proof of the staying
power of dancers in our so-called "marathon" dances, in
which competing couples hold the floor through an almost unbelievable number of hours.

But dance affects not only the performer; the observer
also is influenced. By its incessant and regular recurrence,
rhythm takes a ruthless hold on the attention, forcing
even the most recalcitrant to yield to its spell. The sight of
pulsative movement makes the observer feel emotion
similar to that experienced by the performer, for by imagination he dances with him. "As evidence of the irresisti-
bility with which a rhythmical expression may rouse an
audience to an almost unvoluntary imitation," says Yrjö
Hirn in The Origins of Art, "one may refer to the south-
ern dances. The tarantella, as is well known, often entices
the unwilling as well as the willing to join in its wild
movements. And the same is said of several other Spanish
and Italian dances. We need only refer to the apologue
of the Fandango, so often used as a motive of ballets,
in which the dance, brought into court for causing dis-
turbance, compels judge and jury to yield to its tempta-
tions and dissolve the sitting for a fierce gambade. Such
stories give an exaggerated yet typical example of the great

THE ARTIST'S TRANSLATION OF REALITY

Above, *Weather-beaten*, a painting by Winslow Homer. Below, the actual scene at Prout's Neck, Maine, which served as model. The artist did more than make a photographic likeness of his subject. He selected, arranged, and heightened certain features for effect.

THE TRANSLATION OF REALITY ON THE STAGE

The raw material (below) and the dramatic translation of this material in a stage performance (above). A scene from *New Nigger*, by Fred Howard, produced by the Carolina Playmakers.

influence which the sight of dancing exercises on the lively
Latin nations. An impassive Northerner can indeed always master the impulse to join actively in a wild dance.
But even he cannot avoid sharing the excitement by internal imitation." [6] A suspicion that the impassive northerner is not always such a master of his impulses as Mr.
Hirn maintains is raised by the behavior of many bystand-
ers at jazz balls and jazz concerts.

THE INFLUENCE OF SINGING

If dancing leads to exhilaration and ecstasy, so does singing. And the basic reason why song may so powerfully
affect the human organism is that all musical tone is
stimulating. Psychological experiments made on listeners
have shown that music causes a number of biological
changes. It effects an alteration in pulse, respiration, and
external blood pressure. It delays muscular fatigue and
increases metabolism. It lowers the threshold of sensitivity to other forms of stimulation. In other words, music
sets up in the body the precise changes which psychology
has long recognized as the physiological substrata of emotion. It stirs up the whole man, physically as well as mentally.[7]

The neural connections between the ear and the higher
nervous centers constitute a larger part of the human
brain than those of any other sense. The ear is the re-
ceptor organ most closely associated with the general ori-
entation of the body. Besides responding to sound, it is

directly connected with the sense of balance and direction upon which the control of movement depends. Musical tone is therefore intimately associated with man's feeling of bodily action and control. The human organism is unique in this respect. In none of the animals, not even the higher primates, does the ear occupy such a central place in the adjustment of the organism to its environment. Consequently, music, especially when it involves the human voice, is one of the most powerful stimulants in the whole perceptual experience of man.

Because musical tones are capable of exerting such a stirring influence on movement and emotion, they have long served a utilitarian purpose. Singing serves the primitive man not only for his recreational and religious activities, but also to energize him for all his necessary labors. The greatest foe of the savage is not beast, man, or the forces of nature. It is his own mental and physical inertia. Largely unaffected by those far-reaching desires for wealth, softer living conditions, social advancement, power, which spur civilized peoples to action, the savage tends to lead a will-less existence, putting off from day to day the chores connected with his livelihood. An historian of the eighteenth century who describes American Indians he had observed tells of their fondness for hunting, but their distaste for any other form of labor. "They never work as the English do," he remarks, "taking care for no farther than what is absolutely necessary to support life." [8] Students of primitive people elsewhere have noted the same tendency. This sluggish, will-less inertia is called *aboulia* and represents a real menace to the planting of crops and other routine and nonroutine work. A

principal weapon against inactivity is singing. Primitive
man sings to stir himself for tasks in the field, for row-
ing boats, for carrying loads, and especially for war and
courtship.

But primitive man is not the only one who has felt the
practical value of tone play. Nearly all civilized peoples

EVERYBODY SINGS
Singing produces vitality, a sense of well-being.

have used songs as aids to work. The Greeks had songs for
harvesting, grain grinding, wine making, drawing of water,
spinning, weaving, and dyeing. Craftsmen in the Philip-
pines, in Borneo, India, Siam, Japan, and Korea, work to

the accompaniment of songs. Arabs sing while tending
camels and shearing sheep. Chinese sing while repairing
streets, fighting fires, bearing burdens, working metals,
building houses. In this country, Negro stevedores and
cotton pickers move to music. Music both vocal and
instrumental, found to be a practical stimulant to activity, is now used regularly in a number of North American industries. Piano or phonograph selections are employed in many modern business schools to control and
accelerate the speed of typists and penmen.[9]

The exhilarating effect produced upon the human organism by song and dancelike band music is readily observed at athletic gatherings. Organized cheering is only
a slightly altered form of the savage war dance. Without
the whipping-up given by the singing, band playing, and
cheering, most of our university football games would
probably be rather unexciting events. The forced stimulation affects not only the spectators, but also the players,
driving them to superhuman feats of daring, speed, and
strength.

How musical tones can activate the behavior of soldiers
has been demonstrated countless times. Chieftains have
led their forces to the attack, singing. The fife and drum
have helped to win many battles. The trumpet and bugle
have spurred warriors to numberless charges. The effect
of the bagpipes on Scottish Highlanders has been recorded again and again. There is an old saying that the
Hungarian troops are the worst in Europe until their
bands begin to play. Then they are the best. The late General Linevitch is quoted as declaring that "music is one
of the most vital ammunitions of the Russian Army.

Without music a Russian soldier would be dull, cowardly, brutal and inefficient. From music he absorbs a magic power of endurance, and forgets the sufferings and mortality. It is a divine dynamite." [10] Organized singing has been exploited also very successfully among German fighting troops.

That the effects produced by dancelike and songlike music on laborers, athletes, and soldiers are directly active, and not dependent solely on associations, as some maintain, is proved by the fact that feeble-minded people, even idiots, and animals are stirred to movement by it. Responses have been observed in spiders, fish, rats, mice, pigs, seals, and birds. Snakes, it is said, are charmed by musical tones, especially those rendered on a flute. Elephants are sensitive, behaving in different ways to different kinds of music.[11] It has been a custom among the Arabs from very early times to encourage camels on the march by the chanting of verse.[12] Cattle are controlled by cowboys' songs. Dogs are particularly susceptible to tone play. Nearly everyone who has observed the behavior of a dog that enters a room where people are singing or playing the piano will remember the sudden lifting of the nose and the consequent howl. Even when dogs do not respond vocally, they tend to be nervous, scratching themselves, lying close to the ground and raising and lowering their heads, or retiring under a piece of furniture in a highly excited condition. That most of them enjoy the music is shown by the fact that they choose to remain near the source of tone.

The conclusion that it is not so much the word as the tone which supplies the entrancing influence of song comes also from an investigation of early poems and chants. Many of these are made up of quite meaningless syllables. Examples of these wordless poems and chants have been found in primitive tribes of Africa, South America, and the polar regions. When words are used, the order is often distorted for the sake of sound and rhythm. Most of the songs of the Australian aborigines, the Mincopies, and other simple peoples, are quite meaningless to all but the singers. In some Eskimo songs the text is merely a repetition of meaningless interjections. Refrains of senseless syllables are characteristic of primitive songs in general.[13]

Songs with meaningless words are daily proving their tonal power in our own churches. The chanting of the priest in the Roman Catholic service is in Latin, and the cantillation in the Orthodox Jewish synagogue is in Hebrew, both languages unfamiliar to most of the congregation. In many other kinds of church services, the tone is equal to, if not more important than, the word. The arrangement of most anthems offers a good example. The songlike exhortation of the preacher, and the group hymns and prayer chants at "revival" meetings, often depend very little on intellectual content for their spellbinding effect. It is the tone, intensified where possible by convulsive, dancelike movement, which leads to ecstasy. The same thing may be said for jazz, for its methods are not far removed from those of many religious rituals. "The rising frenzy of the Negro ring shout and the voluptuous ecstasies of the jazz ball," says Isaac Goldberg in *Tin Pan Alley*, "are sisters under the skin." [14]

DANCE, SONG, AND MAGIC

Nothing manifests so clearly, perhaps, the activating power of the dance pulse and the singing tone as the history of magic.

The mythologies of nearly every country in the world contain figures of gods and demigods to whom was ascribed miraculous ability as musicians. In the Greek legends there are Tyrtaeus, who aroused an army to action by means of a flute; Terpander, who with a similar instrument restored a rebellious people to allegiance; Amphion, who raised the walls of Thebes with the playing of his lyre; Arion, who, thrown into the sea by pirates, was rescued by dolphins charmed by the music of his lyre. The best-known figure is that of Orpheus. His song subdued wild beasts, arrested the course of waves, made trees and rocks

PLAINS INDIAN DOG DANCER
A performer in a religious ceremonial dance. (After Bodmer.)

dance. When his beloved wife, Eurydice, died, he descended into Hades, charmed the creatures of the underworld, and won from Pluto himself the temporary release of his wife. The legend of Orpheus is world-wide. There are Gaelic, Hindu, and even Hawaiian Orpheuses. In Hindu myths, singers influence the growth of plants, change the course of the seasons, stop the sun, cause rain to fall. Irish myths contain references to miraculous harps, whistles, and horns. Scotch and Welsh folk stories tell of spells cast on various people by music. In Frankish legends the horn of the paladin Roland is endowed with magical powers. The horn of Huon of Bordeaux makes listeners dance.[15] Prussian legends contain the famous tale of the Pied Piper of Hamelin and his power over rats and children. The Bible tells us that the walls of Jericho fell when priests blew blasts on their trumpets. Saul was cured of his sickness by David's harp, and Solomon was driven to folly by the songs of his wives. Greek and Teutonic mariners were lured to their deaths by the sweet singing of sirens.

Many of these early stories doubtless had their origins in the magical practices of tribal priests. The relationship between dancing, singing, and magic can be observed in the medicine men of primitive people today. The technique of these men shows the powerful spell-casting influence of organized pulse and tone on both the performer and his spectator. The medicine man, or the conjurer, works to create a sense of omnipotence in thought and will. He knows that this sense is strongest when the human organism is in a dynamic condition. Dancing and chanting, he has learned, help to evoke powerful movements of the organism with a consequent feeling of unlimited might. So he uses music constantly with his magic; and feats of magic in turn become associated with the

Armand Denis–Universal Films

PRIMITIVE DANCE

A dance of the Watusi giants, as recorded in *Dark Rapture*, a documentary film made in the Belgian Congo.

Armand Denis–Universal Films

A MODERN VERSION OF THE PRIMITIVE DANCE

A chorus dance from *The Hot Mikado*.

force of music. "Man can work magic when dehumanized, transported, lifted by the divine out of the everyday, torn out of the normal path of life, he walks into the void, into that expanse where the self mingles with the infinite. Out of his transport a mastery over spirits grows in him; a power to work in conjunction with the superman, to take control over the events of which his daily life is a part." [16] That is the magic of the dancer and singer.

PULSATIVE MOVEMENT, TONE, AND PATTERN

Much of the dancing and of the singing described in the preceding sections is of an exceptionally energetic type— dancing marked by fast, strong accents, and singing characterized by lively inflection and tempo. That accent, inflection, and tempo exert a powerful influence for excitement cannot be denied. But the person who is investigating the dramatic values of dance and song should recognize first that the primary effects lie in factors more basic: simple pulsative movement and simple musical tone.

Psychological experiments have shown that gay and "stirring" songs are not alone in their stimulating influence on the human organism. Grave, and even tranquil, music produces similar physiological changes. This fact, among others, shows that the basic quality of music lies more in tone than in structural relationships or connotative symbolism. A song of indifferent composition and in a foreign

tongue, but sung by a richly vibrant voice, can affect a
listener with deeper emotion than the most perfectly constructed song in English if it is rendered by an inferior
voice. Tone is the magical agent.[17]

Likewise in dancing, it is not the shape, time, or extent
of movement which is of primary significance, but the

THE BALLERINA

The movements of classical ballet are restricted mostly to the legs
and arms.

fundamental pulse beat. Many of the most potent dances
of the East are done with the feet held quite motionless.
Among our own dances, the one form which has kept an
unbroken popularity for nearly two hundred years while
scores of other more frolicsome steps have come and
gone, is the form which, while it involves a certain sweep
of movement, is based on the slowest time figure—the

waltz. The insistent force of the pulse beat is what counts most.

However, basic as tone and pulse are to the emotive effect of singing and dancing, it would be a mistake to intimate that they alone are important. There is a third

MODERN DANCERS

The modern dance is a highly exacting form which requires the use, not of the legs and arms only, but of the whole body. Martha Graham's Group, sketched by Betty Joiner. (Reproduced by courtesy of *Theatre Arts Monthly*.)

agent only a little less influential than the first two. That is pattern. While tone and pulse beat create *general* feelings in the auditor and spectator, pattern produces *specific* feelings. Because of pattern in the dance, we recognize and respond differently to the tap step and the waltz; to the movements of a revue chorus and those of a ballet. Because of pattern in song, we vary our reactions from one composition to another. A dirgelike tune will cause a response quite different from one designed for a call to battle—even when we do not have the words. Solo singing produces an emotion quite unlike that given by voices in harmony.

While pulse beat and tone singly affect the involuntary processes of the body, patterns of these stir also the voluntary musculature and exert a very important influence on all kinds of human action. Elements of dance pattern are time, space, and force; those of song are time, pitch, and force. Both forms are inflected (line of movement, and melody); both are controlled by laws of harmony; and both are built from smaller units to larger by means of architectonic design.

DANCING AS
AN EXPRESSION OF EMOTION

Dancing and singing, possessing as they do strongly activating properties in respect to the human organism, become naturally in turn the most expressive reflections of man's emotional urges. Man dances and sings to give vent to his feelings. Rhythmical movement and rhythmical song speak directly of his inner desires and his dreams.

Man shares with the animals these twin avenues of emotive expression. All kinds of insects, birds, and other creatures sing constantly about their feelings. And many of the animals dance. Rabbits, skunks, porcupines, and

A DANCE FORM OF TODAY

Fred Astaire in the film *Top Hat*. The picture emphasizes the off-the-earth spirit of this popular dancer.

Hansen-Pavelle

BALLET

From *Les Sylphides*, a "romantic reverie," presented by the Monte Carlo Ballet Russe.

turkeys prance rhythmically. And there are reports of
dancing mountain cocks in British Guiana, and of os-
triches who beat time with their wings while they twirl
round and round with breathless rapidity.[18] A coconut
planter on an island near Cape York in northeastern Aus-
tralia describes the dance of the stiltbirds:

"The birds, of a kind known locally as Native Companions, were long-legged creatures, tall almost as storks,
and white and grey of feather; and the dance took place
in the center of a broad, dry swamp, from the edge of
which, in a place of concealment, we watched. There
were some hundreds of them, and their dance was in the
manner of quadrille, but in the matter of rhythm and
grace excelling any quadrille that ever was. In groups
of a score or more they advanced and retreated, lifting
their long legs and standing on their toes, now and then
bowing gracefully one to another, now and then one
pair encircling with prancing daintiness a group whose
heads moved upwards and downwards and sidewise in
time to the stepping of the pair. At times they formed
into one great prancing mass, with their long necks
thrust upward; and the wide swaying of their backs was
like unto the swaying of the sea. Then, suddenly, as in
response to an imperative command, they would sway
apart, some of them to rise in low, encircling flight, and
some to stand as in little gossiping groups; and presently
they would form in pairs or sets of pairs, and the prancing and the bowing, and advancing and retreating would
begin all over again." [19]

One of the most interesting documents dealing with
animal behavior comes from the laboratory for the study

of anthropoid apes in Teneriffe, where a number of chimpanzees with no former contact with human beings were brought up under scientific observation. The psychologist, Wolfgang Köhler, who for six years was in charge of the laboratory, reports at some length to the Prussian Academy of Science how apes dance. He tells of solo dances, and of group dances in a circle, with the apes stepping rhythmically, often spinning on their own axes, round and round a post in the center. Summing up the generally emotional behavior of his chimpanzees, Köhler remarks: "The chimpanzee's register of emotional expression is so much greater than that of average human beings, because his whole body is agitated and not merely his facial muscles. He jumps up and down both in joyful anticipation and in impatient annoyance and anger; and in extreme despair—which develops under very slight provocation—flings himself on his back and rolls wildly to and fro. He also swings and waves his arms about above his head in a fantastic manner." [20]

Surely in the chimpanzee's emotional behavior may be seen rudiments of the dance. To say, as Köhler does, that the chimpanzee's register is so much greater than that of human beings is to take into consideration only the actions of more controlled persons. Children and savages in moments of high emotion express themselves not very differently from these apes.

From the dance movements of the highest animals to those of primitive man is one step, though a long one. In the dances of the savage, performed by a single body or in groups, are found the same convulsive jerks, hoppings, prances, and whirlings. Done, however, for some-

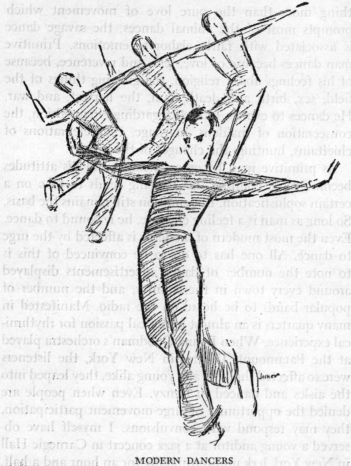

MODERN DANCERS

Exhibition dancing in primitive communities is performed chiefly by men. Any participation in this form of dancing in civilized societies has long been viewed with suspicion by the more masculine elements. Only recently in this country has dancing become again a manly occupation. Charles Weidman's Group, sketched by Betty Joiner. (Reproduced by courtesy of *Theatre Arts Monthly*.)

thing more than the pure love of movement which prompts most of the animal dances, the savage dance is associated with fairly elaborate emotions. Primitive man dances because of love, fear, and reverence, because of his feelings about religion, the growing things of the field, sex, birth and death, rain, the harvest, and war. He dances to express himself regarding circumcision, the consecration of maidens, marriage, the celebrations of chieftains, hunting, the changes of the moon.

As primitive man becomes civilized and his attitudes become more complex, his dancing tends to take on a certain sophistication. But emotion still remains the basis. So long as man is a feeling creature, he is bound to dance. Even the most modern of moderns is affected by the urge to dance. All one has to do to be convinced of this is to note the number of dance advertisements displayed around every town in the country, and the number of popular bands to be heard on the radio. Manifested in many quarters is an almost hysterical passion for rhythmical experience. When Benny Goodman's orchestra played at the Paramount Theatre in New York, the listeners were so affected that, old and young alike, they leaped into the aisles and danced in frenzy. Even when people are denied the opportunity of large-movement participation, they may respond with convulsions. I myself have observed a young auditor at a jazz concert in Carnegie Hall in New York jerk uninterruptedly for an hour and a half, stopping only during the intervals between numbers.

Broadly speaking, however, all the intense activity connected with the ballroom gives modern man only a limited outlet for his dancing urge. In comparison with the savage, the present-day sophisticate, with his innumerable taboos against excess movement, leads emotionally a bottled-up existence. Joy he may express only through a smile; repugnance, with a frown. Fear and grief he may not show at all, except through neutral words. Any visual

MODERN DANCERS

Modern dancers are trained athletes with strong, flexible bodies. Hanya Holm's Group, sketched by Betty Joiner. (Reproduced by courtesy of *Theatre Arts Monthly*.)

hint of wonderment in the presence of the awe-inspiring is forbidden. Ecstasy must never be manifest. Why? Because it is "unmannerly." It interferes with the sense of the efficiently predictable in men's relationships with other men. Largely on account of this social setting-of-the-lid on natural inclinations to work emotions out of the system through expressive movement, we see today widespread nervous disorders; and on the other hand we see

the extraordinary interest in stage dancing. From the
forms of the ballet, and even from the chorus numbers of
popular revues, observers derive a vicarious release for
their pent-up urges.

Revue dancing, which is commonly more spectacular
than dynamic, offers less of the outlet here described than
does ballet. The latter forms are aimed more directly at
expressiveness than are the first. But even in the expressive
forms a strong distinction must be drawn. It is not the
traditional forms of the past century which have the most
lasting appeal now, for the design of the so-called "classical ballet" of the nineteenth century was pretty artificial
and static. The greater stimulation lies in the new figures
inspired by Isadora Duncan's free dances and worked out
for the "reformed ballet" by such artists as Nijinski and
Fokine. This kind of dancing we see today in the work
of the Ballet Russe, the Jooss Ballet, the Ballet Caravan,
and others.

But the most effective forms of all are those which
have broken entirely with the traditional ballet. Such
artists in America as Martha Graham, Doris Humphrey,
Charles Weidman, and Hanya Holm are exploring once
more the simple, primitive urge to move rhythmically,
and at the same time they are trying to express through
these movements basic emotions in contemporary American life.

DANCE IN DRAMATIC FORM

Two scenes from Jacob Prager's folk comedy, *The Water Carrier*, as produced by the Yiddish Art Theatre in New York. Sketched by Betty Joiner. (Reproduced by courtesy of *Theatre Arts Monthly*.)

SINGING AS
AN EXPRESSION OF EMOTION

Man sings for the same reason that he dances—to express his emotion. The song of the savage may be crude; it may be limited to a few simple intervals set in monotonous rhythms. The tonal quality may, for trained ears, lack richness and brilliance. But the song reflects the feelings of the man who sings. To his ears, and to the ears of his primitive listeners, it is sweet music. It expresses fully his joys and his sorrows, and in his listeners it stirs the same longing, fear, and hope which impelled him to sing.

As human life becomes more complicated in the higher

levels of civilization, it demands more and more refinement in its expressive channels. But song remains a fundamental medium. Wherever man is free to utter his passions, he sings. He sings when he is happy; he sings when he is sad. He sings when he loves, when he hates, when he is exalted, depressed, restless, and at peace. He sings to express his feelings about religion, about birth, about courtship, marriage, and death. He sings in every kind of condition—when he is free.

In "civilized" surroundings man must constantly curb his singing. But the impulse is there. He finds some compensation for his long periods of silence by engaging occasionally in "barber-shop harmonizing" with his friends, intoning hymns in church, and singing in his bath. Usually, however, these few blessed moments of release are insufficient. So we are compelled to sing vicariously through the songs of others, men and women who are trained to express, even better than we can ourselves, our deep-lying pain, hunger, and joy. This explains in great part the popularity of the radio, the phonograph, the opera, and the concert stage. There *must* be expression through song, for man is a singing animal.

DANCING, SINGING, AND ACTING

To sum up, dancing and singing perform two great human functions: they stimulate the body and mind into action, and they offer channels of release for man's inward feeling. Their natural powers in these two fields are unlimited. Dancing and singing are imbued with magic.

Because of their profoundly stimulating and eloquent qualities, elements of dance and song may be used to advantage in the player's art. They are powerful factors for dramatic effect.

Chapter Three

THE PLAYER
DANCING

DANCE AND SONG:
A COMPARISON

Dramatic design, as we have observed, is like musical design in that at the heart of each lie dancing and singing. Viewed in their purest aspects, the element of dance is pulsative, dynamic, while the element of song is lyrical. One is a step, or a leap; the other a cry. Dance is always positively physical. Singing, though it never lacks a physical basis, has also, often, a contemplative side. Dancing springs from the impulse to *do*, song from the urge to *feel*.

The basic difference between dance and song in music is illustrated in the two old English tunes on page 42, "Green Sleeves," and "O Death! Rock Me Asleep," ascribed to Anne Boleyn. Even when one disregards the words, one sees readily that the first, with its insistent pulse beat, is primarily a dance; the second, with its emphasis on tone rather than meter, is pre-eminently a song.

DANCE TUNE

From "Green Sleeves," an Elizabethan air.

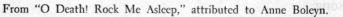

SONG TUNE

From "O Death! Rock Me Asleep," attributed to Anne Boleyn.

But the elements of dancing and singing practically never appear singly except in primitive forms. The first of the two tunes, "Green Sleeves," was composed for lyrical expression as well as pulsative movement, and "O Death! Rock Me Asleep" has—unobtrusive though it may be—a rhythm influenced by dancing. The well-

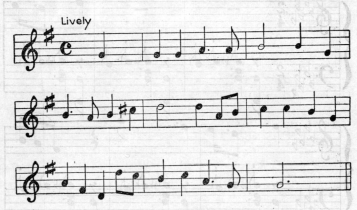

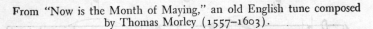

DANCE AND SONG COMBINED

From "Now is the Month of Maying," an old English tune composed by Thomas Morley (1557–1603).

known little Elizabethan air above, "Now is the Month of Maying," shows dance and song indissolubly united.

For the manner in which dance and song co-operate to produce a singleness of expression in instrumental music, one finds an example on page 44 in the selection from the second movement of Tchaikovsky's string quartet, Opus 11. See how the treble notes carry a wandering, lyrical cry, while the bass swings out a steady, measured

dance. In many more closely knit compositions the two
elements of music cannot be so easily separated and
analyzed; but they are both there.

The modern concert song, and even the modern concert dance, are not pure forms. The song is always modi-

DANCE AND SONG IN INSTRUMENTAL MUSIC

A passage from the second movement, "Andante cantabile," of Tchaikovsky's string quartet, Opus 11.

fied by the rhythms of dance steps; and most of the dancing is touched by the lyricism of song. All slow dancing
—in contrast to the quick, convulsive, leaping movements
of the savage—is, in a measure, songlike. If the popular
"swing" song is affected by dancing, the waltz—often
used as a vehicle for ballads—is influenced by singing.
By analogy, when the elements of dance and song appear in the art of the actor, we must realize that they do
not appear in pure states, singly. Rhythmical pantomime
is almost always associated with musical speech, even
when no word is uttered, and vice versa.

It is not really necessary to hold the ideas of pulsative
movement and the lyrical cry distinctly apart in our minds
while we are considering the two branches of acting. For
general convenience, to keep the broad concepts of dance
and song as simple as possible, we shall assume that pulsative and lyrical aspects are necessarily blended, and refer
to the "dance" as that combination of these two which
finds its field of influence in visual pantomime, whereas
"song," also a blend, operates in aural speech.

We shall consider first the dancing. But before we do
that we must clarify briefly for ourselves the meaning of

THE MEANING
OF RHYTHM

Any investigation of the dancer's technique begins naturally with a study of rhythm. Viewed basically, rhythm
is a pulsation. It is an inherent part of nearly everything

with which we deal. It is everywhere around and within us. From the smallest to the greatest, from the raindrops falling on a blade of grass to the winds that roar across the continent, all dynamic and mutatory existence is affected by pulse beats. There are vibration, oscillation, periodic occurrences and recurrences, in many different patterns—direct rhythms, indirect rhythms, infinitely compounded rhythms—in the air, the earth, the sea.

The wind strikes across the face of the ocean. The waves roll. Over the surface of each wave flutter smaller waves, broken in turn by still smaller ripples. Below the waves march the swells, the rhythm of whose periods is compounded by the movements of the currents. And below them all swing the tides.

On the upper plain of the ocean a ship rolls and tosses, its sail, yards, and cordage, even under the steadiest of breezes, vibrating. The whole ship trembles. But the measure of the trembling differs infinitely from that of the wide movement of the ship in the water. On land, the trees sway slowly, while the leaves, timed to a much faster period, twist and turn. The tall grass beneath the tree and the grain in the neighboring field undulate in the same kind of complex rhythm as the waves of the sea.

Light rays and sound projections are periodic in nature. So also are practically all other cosmic phenomena. Consider, in its larger aspects, the motion of our world and the measurement of time—night and day, the seasons, the years, the decades, the centuries, and the millenniums. The earth rotates on its axis once every twenty-four hours, and it rolls around the sun every twelve months. This

Thomas Bouchard

THE DANCER'S POSSESSION OF SPACE
Martha Graham in her dance *Frontier*.

Margaret DeM. Brown

THE ACTOR'S POSSESSION OF SPACE

The declaration of the dictator in Ernst Toller's *No More Peace*, presented by the Experimental Theatre at Vassar College.

compound motion, we are told, is compounded by still others. The axis of the earth describes in space a figure independent of its simpler movement in the annual orbit, a figure which is repeated once every 26,000 years. And yet the vast rhythm of our planet does not end there, for it is observed that the whole complex solar system to which the earth belongs is traveling through space presumably in a closed circuit, the length of which cannot be appraised by human minds.

The law of recurring intervals, which governs the movement of inanimate objects, affects especially the animate. Life is the expression of rhythms, myriads of throbbings, great and small. The pulsing of the blood, the measured action of the respiratory and digestive systems, the alternating constrictive and relaxant behavior of the locomotor muscles, the periodic need of food, exercise, and rest—are all readily observable phenomena. Man's mental functions are influenced by similar laws of interval. Consider his recurring moods, his moments of attention and inattention, his hopes and fears, and the bearing these have on the behavior of society—eras of activity and passivity, commercial cycles, fluctuating markets, literary and other "movements," periods of prosperity, national enthusiasms and depressions. The principles which regulate the life and death of man as an individual reach ultimately to the rising and falling of civilizations.

Simple periodicity lies at the center of rhythm. But it is not all of rhythm. The uniform ticking of a clock is just a repetition. Rhythm, in the broad sense, involves the grouping of beats into patterns. The diagrams on page 49 illustrate the difference between simple repetition and real rhythm.

Modern psychology defines the human sense of rhythm as "an instinctive disposition to group recurrent sense impressions vividly and with precision, by time, or intensity, or both, in such a way as to derive pleasure and efficiency through the grouping." [1] The process is a complicated one, often involving the physical as well as the mental side of a man's organism. Practically, the sense of rhythm is of two kinds, objective and subjective. The objective kind is the apprehension of natural or artificial patterns which are already formed, like those in music. The subjective kind is the grouping of beats which are absolutely uniform in time and intensity, taking them as if they were actually patterned. The mind does the grouping. Nearly everyone lying in a Pullman sleeper has been struck by the musical measures which the wheels passing over the rail joints seem to form in one's ear.

The subjective sense of rhythm is the more fundamental, and it lies beneath our keen appreciation of the objective rhythms in art. This is because the disposition to group is part of our natural processes. We think, we feel, we act, rhythmically. Rhythm is a biological principle of efficiency. For this reason, visual and vocal stimuli which are already formed into group patterns fall rapidly into the perception and comprehension of the observer. The psychological mechanism is already set for it.

For anyone who doubts the validity of this statement there are two simple experiments. Let him have a friend read a page from this or any other book in a monotone

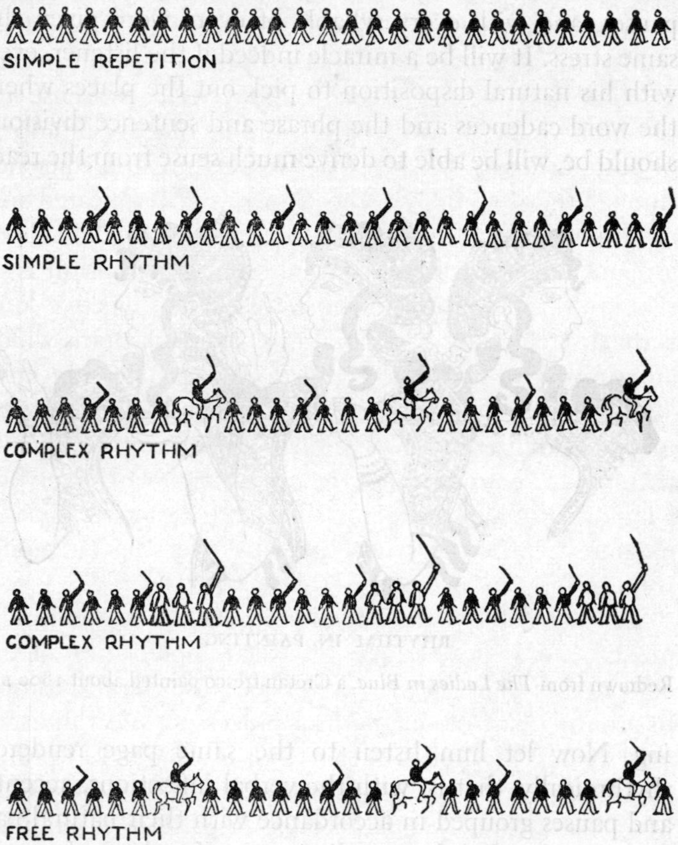

SIMPLE REPETITION

SIMPLE RHYTHM

COMPLEX RHYTHM

COMPLEX RHYTHM

FREE RHYTHM

RHYTHM

Repetition and real rhythm. Fixed—simple and complex—and free
forms. The figures with raised sticks represent the accents.

and at an absolutely uniform rate of speed, with no pauses, and with every syllable of every word given the same stress. It will be a miracle indeed if the listener, even with his natural disposition to pick out the places where the word cadences and the phrase and sentence divisions should be, will be able to derive much sense from the read-

RHYTHM IN PAINTING

Redrawn from *The Ladies in Blue*, a Cretan fresco painted about 1800 B.C.

ing. Now let him listen to the same page rendered rhythmically, that is, with the verbal inflections, accents, and pauses grouped in accordance with their natural patterns. Or let the observer listen to a few bars of music, first without and then with the measured beats indicated for it. The value of the periodic groupings should become apparent at once. Experiments with color spots, lines, and other shapes will show similar tendencies in the visual field.

When we refer to a "dance rhythm," then, we are not speaking of something composed, by either a primitive or a sophisticated artist, apart from contact with daily living. Rhythm is a central element of biology. We depend on rhythm to feel, to think, to move, to project ourselves effectively. We also depend on rhythm to perceive, to respond efficiently to outside stimuli. Because rhythm is such a basic part of our whole physical, mental, and spiritual being, and our welfare depends on it, we rejoice in the *sense* of rhythm. The dance is a flowering of rhythmical impulses, intensified and ordered for maximum effect.

The following points we have now established about dancing. It is pulsative. The beats are ordered into group patterns, either mathematically regulated, or quite free like the waves on the ocean. There are accented beats, and lesser beats. And there are moments of pause (or lesser tension) to punctuate the phrases of action. Most important of all, every bit of this activity is related to human personality.

THE DANCER IN THE ACTOR

Doubtless most of the readers of this book accept the idea that rhythm has a dramatic value. But some of them may find it difficult to admit that stage pantomime should be "dancelike." Enjoying the dance well enough in its place, they feel nevertheless (mistakenly, I believe) that too much association between it and acting tends to destroy

in acting that dignified reticence which is now so generally admired. This attitude arises from a rather limited
conception of what dancing may be.

It is true that much of the movement seen on the contemporary stage—in the stilted jumping and attitudiniz-
ing of traditional ballet on one hand and in the almost
formless one-two-three kicking of popular chorus work
on the other—exerts only a distant influence on acting.
But there are other kinds of dancing. For the benefit of
those who are in doubt with regard to our point of view
in this book let it be strongly emphasized here that we
have in mind none of the more extravagant types. The
kind of movement to which we wish to relate the best of
acting employs no cheese cloth or fluttering wrists. It
abhors fancy posing and gracefulness exploited for itself
alone. The dancing which serves as foundation for dramatic pantomime is based on free, strong, full-bodied
action. It is the kind of dancing which springs from the
movements of natural walking, the stepping, thrusting,
and dodging of the boxer in the ring, the running and
throwing of the ball-player, the hoeing, plowing, and
chopping of the man in the fields. It is fundamentally as
manly, and womanly, as is daily life.

When dance is viewed in connection with dramatic
pantomime, the relationship must, of course, be seen
broadly. It is not the fixed steps, or gestures, of the dancer
which the actor employs to create effect, but the inner
essence of the dance; that is, pulsative movement,
grouped, accented, and composed in space. Bound, as
he is, to keep *characterization* in the foreground of the
spectator's attention, the player is usually forced to hide,

or disguise, the rhythmical devices of his art. Very occasionally he has an opportunity to work directly, as in episodes of such plays as O'Casey's *Within the Gates*, Sundgaard and Connelly's *Everywhere I Roam*, and Green's *The Lost Colony*, in which the movement of human character grows and blossoms into pure dance. But such moments in modern plays are rare. Usually the actor must strive to produce his stimulative and expressive effects still rhythmically, but more subtly.

The three factors of dance design are, as already indicated, time, space, and force. As we consider the dramatic player's use of pulsative movement in the following pages, we should think of it in connection with these three.

TIME DANCING IN ACTING

The time factor of dancing is made up of two things: rhythm and the pace of this rhythm, tempo. If an investigation of the actor's technique begins at this point, it may run immediately into an objection on the part of the reader. "Is stimulative and expressive playing necessarily pulsative?" he may ask. "For certain kinds of representation, perhaps. But for all? I doubt it."

Let us start with poetic drama. Anyone who has seen a really light-footed performance of a verse comedy—*As You Like It*, for example—will readily admit, I believe, that here rhythmical movement is an important part of the visual interpretation. To fulfill the spirit of their dialogue lines, the characters must move with agility, swiftly, neatly, in time with definite pulse beats, poised at every moment for nimble thrust, retreat, and merry counter-thrust, in wide patterns of individual and group design. Here, surely, is dance, not very much disguised. Even in the prose parts of these comedies the players' actions must maintain a swing—freer, perhaps, but definitely rhythmical. As soon as the pantomime jerks, plods, or stands still, the spirit and the thought of the play are destroyed, even if, which is unlikely, the lines continue to be well delivered. Without the contribution of the dancelike movement, the visual side of the play is unanimated.

In the performance of a verse tragedy, wherein dialogue rhythm is slower, the visual "dance" must perforce be more stately, dignified, than in the comedy just mentioned. Sometimes the pantomime movement demanded in certain parts of plays like *Macbeth, Hamlet,* or *Pelléas and Mélisande* is so very deliberate that the observer may fail to appreciate in it the underlying pulsation. But taking into mind the rhythmical demands of all the verse scenes considered collectively, nearly everyone will agree that dance, viewed broadly, has a central place in the effect. Pulsative speech must be accompanied by pulsative action.

Many interpretations of the classics, especially the Greek plays with their choral movements, demand an equally frank use of dance pantomime. In the performances of these plays and all the foregoing dramas, the place of the dance is clear. Pulsation is a part of the open fiber of the playwright's own design. The actor and the director cannot reasonably do anything else than follow the pattern. However, the value of rhythmic movement for the realistic, prose type of play is not always so evident.

For the person who has never before regarded the question of rhythm in "realism," it should prove helpful to consider the silent motion pictures, in the preparation of which pantomime was rehearsed to music. Measured melodies were used, partly to build a mood in the actors, but more directly to help them establish a rhythm for their work. Experience in recording their actions through the throbbing eye of the camera showed that movements unprompted by music tended to be jumpy, and therefore inexpressive. So the orchestra was used freely. Numbers were selected to fit the measured, or dancelike, character of each "shot," and to them the actions of the players were keyed. There were waltz scenes, march scenes, two-step scenes, all carefully rehearsed for precise timing. Worked out in this way, the pantomime acquired the qualities, not only of smoothness and flow, but also of development, magnitude, and completeness that would have been difficult to achieve otherwise. Thus, the best of the pantomime in silent films reached a very high level of eloquence—without the aid of words.

With the coming of the talking pictures, and the recording of dialogue, the orchestra had to be removed from the set. But, although the actors now had to perform without music, they had to play for music. There is scarcely a reputable film released today that does not carry at least some melodic and rhythmical accompaniment. The most memorable films are usually extensively underscored. Although the actors no longer rehearse to the time beat by an orchestra, they carefully plan their performance so that the *effect* is the same. Now it is not the player who hears the music, but the spectator.

That element of stage acting termed by us "dancing" is closely akin to the music-prompted movements just described. The bodily actions with which it is identified are free and large, economical—that is, with no waste exertion; and, being rhythmical, they are marked by periodic motion, periodic rest, and periodic points of special stress. They are rehearsed by the player in the theatre without actual music, since this is not readily obtainable there, and because the scenes through which the player moves are too long and involved to make an intimate accompaniment practical. Besides, the actor must talk through his pantomime. However, every rightly trained actor goes through his motions, sitting, rising, walking, gesturing, *as if there were music present.* His spirit dances to rhythms heard by the ears of his mind; as a result his outward body becomes likewise rhythmical. An observer seeing the outward movements of the player notices in them no fixed time patterns, but he senses through the manifest movements the stirring and guiding *influence* of music.

A specific example may help to clarify our meaning of dancing. Take the simple action sequence involved in rising from a chair, walking across the room, lifting a letter from a table, turning and handing it to a person. A player who is not a "dancer" would carry his action through clearly but without much expressive grace. With his feet planted out in front of him, he would probably propel himself into a standing position, and then "make for" the table. The intervening ground might be covered

in a number of different ways, perhaps by jouncing, shuf-
fling, or a sidling movement. Arriving at the table slowly
and uncertainly, the player might suddenly break tempo
again by darting out his hand, seizing the letter, and
thrusting it at his companion. Now observe the trained
actor. He tucks his feet under him to take the weight of
his body in balance, rises quietly, straight up, without
twisting or shooting forward. He rests a short instant after
rising, then walks simply (with no unnecessary bouncing,
wriggling, or hitching) to a point at the table near the
letter (so that he will not have to lean for it), pauses another small fraction of a second, reaches easily for the
sheet of paper, and, turning, presents it to the person waiting for it. The rhythmical time beats of his rising, crossing, reaching, and turning are about the same, with the
rests fitting in. From first to last there is no jerkiness in
the movement, but instead a fine sense of smooth progres-
sion from unit to unit. If the final detail of handing the
note to the other man must be dramatic, it is somewhat
accented, but even this more forceful gesture, like the
rest, is affected by rhythm.

This is, of course, a very simple example. Although it
suggests how the recognition of rhythmical beats may aid
an actor in making his pantomime gracefully effective, it
does not indicate any of the more subtle, genuinely emotional elements of this dramatic dance. On this level,
pulsative movement portrays "efficiency." Thus it is similar to the rhythmical movement of trained athletes.
Much of the training of boxers, runners, rowers, hurdlers,
pole vaulters, hammer and discus throwers, shot putters,
and the like, is a training in rhythm. Long ago the coaches

found that practicing to musical rhythm gives men more speed and strength. This is because rhythm keeps the power flowing smoothly. Without rhythm, athletes, like jerking cars, tend to lunge and relax, lunge and relax. This wastes power. When, out of several hundred track and field events in eleven Olympics, Italian athletes succeeded in winning just four, Premier Mussolini sent to America for a trainer to solve the problem of improved technique. He did solve it—with rhythm.[2]

Rhythmic acting, like rhythmic jumping and throwing, then, is "efficient" acting. But that it may be more than that can easily be demonstrated. In the opening scene of Paul Green's *The House of Connelly*, two old sybil-like Negro women come out to the field to dig for roots by a fence covered with weeds and bushes. They are huge creatures, sexual and fertile, with large breasts and hips, and the muscles of men beneath their old coats. While they dig they chant, about the roots and plants, about the hay poles in the neighboring fields, about the proud General Connelly, and about poor Negro Purvis hanged on the gallows.

BIG SIS. Old General stood up in his long robes and said silence in the court—Purvis to be hung by the neck till dead —and Lord have mercy on your poor soul!—uhm—
BIG SUE. (*Gazing restlessly about her.*) Uhm—yah, and the sky look black same like when they killed the Son o' God.
BIG SIS. Poor Purvis!
BIG SUE. Poor General!
BIG SIS. Own flesh and blood make no difference. The law say hang.
BIG SUE. The General say hang.

BIG SIS. Purvis can't say "pappy."
BIG SUE. General can't say "son," no, Lord, no!
BIG SIS. (*Half musing as she digs.*) Uhm—poor Purvis—
that nigger twist about like a worm on a fishhook the day
they hang him.
BIG SUE. Uhm—din't he? And people everywhere—sitting
on tops of houses like buzzards—uhm—and some of 'em
fainted and fell off when he 'gan wiggle on that rope.
BIG SIS. Old General riding by in his great carriage with
his head bent down.

A gun is fired off far down in the field, and the two
women stop to listen. In unison they make a gesture of
derision in the direction of the ineffectual shooting, laugh,
and then fall back into their digging and chanting.

BIG SUE. Poor nigger. Some of 'em say they hear him
whisper, "Give me some air under this black cap, sweet Lord
Jesus."
BIG SIS. But like the deadfall of the grave they had him
though—Old General Connelly and the law, yeh, had him.
(*Digging furiously.*) Come out of that 'ere ground, old root.
I gwine boil you and drink your sap.
(*She wrenches a root out and hands it up to her sister. The
gun goes off again down in the field.*)
BIG SUE. Shoot them doves, Mr. Will Connelly! You can't
hit 'em and they feets red with blood. Oughter know it.
BIG SIS. Where they trompled in the blood of the Saviour
—nunh-unh.
BIG SUE. Mr. Will couldn't hit 'em if they feets were
black like Satan. (*Big Sis bursts into a peal of laughter.*) Why-
fore?
BIG SIS. (*Straightening up and looking at her sister with
a merry glistening eye.*) He can't shoot. Can't like his pappy.

BIG SUE. (*Laughing till her broad bosom heaves.*) Pop-gun.

BIG SIS. (*Spitting.*) Pop goes the weasel. (*With sudden anger she lifts a huge fist and makes a sweeping gesture over the earth.*) He can't do nothing. Creep about. Let the world rot down. Can't do nothing.

BIG SUE. Yah. (*Softly.*) But Lord, his daddy.

BIG SIS. Old General Connelly was a shooting man. (*She slaps her thigh at some far-off remembrance.*)

BIG SUE. Shoot to kill. (*After a moment—slyly.*) Tu-chu, a hoss-man too and heavy riding man. (*They double over in great gales of laughter.*)

BIG SIS. Yah, and knowed the law. (*Now with sudden mournfulness again.*) But he done gone—gone to his long home.

BIG SUE. (*Forlornly.*) Yah—yah—and the Old Man is there where Purvis is.

BIG SIS. (*Prying among the roots and singing in the deep voice of a man, to which her sister adds a low melodious alto.*)

> In the cold earth the sinful clay
> Wrapped in a sheet is laid away—hah!
> Rock to the hill to trees do mourn
> Pity poor man ever was born—hah! [3]

The directions for the pantomime in this scene are not very specific, and the director and the actors performing it could interpret it in any one of many different ways. But clearly the intention of the playwright would be ignored if the movements of the two Negro women were given without rhythm. Their digging and their pulling among the roots, their heavy actions in filling their baskets, and their gestures to the hay poles, the gun, and other objects in the landscape, are all parts of a lumbering, earthy dance. Without the element of rhythm, the scene would be only half expressed, for Big Sis and Big Sue stand for the swinging, pulsative forces of the fields which the young Will Connelly will never tame.

While this earthy dance is being performed in the fields, a very different dance is taking place in the dining room of the Connelly mansion. With gentle little movements, Will's two spinster sisters are setting the silver on the table, fetching dishes from the kitchen, darting nervously to the window, arranging the decorations. All their actions are small, and nearly all of them are noiseless. These two women also perform a kind of dance, but their dance expresses something very different from the one taking place in the fields. It tells of repressions, aristocratic poverty, deep-lying hungers held for years under the lid of respectability. Without the pulsative, accented movement—pointed up by the sudden lift or closing of a hand, the swift turn of a head, the impulsive shift of the feet—this scene also would be only half expressed.

Not every part of a rhythmical pantomime should be smooth and quiet. Some of it must, of course, be sharp, quick, and vigorous. In the scene in which Will Connelly breaks into rebellion and cries his hatred for the ghosts of Connelly House, he may dance like a savage. The form of each passage is determined by the kind of character performing the dance and the nature of the situation at the point considered. All the action must remain, however, strongly, sensuously rhythmical if it is to be effective.

BURIED RHYTHMS

It may be objected that movements so loosely influenced by pulse beats as those described are not strictly rhythmical. A little consideration of analogous forms, however, will show that the objection cannot be sustained. In a minuet by Mozart the rhythm is obvious. A piano rendition would beat out the time indicated in the signature so clearly that anyone listening could tap it without the slightest difficulty. But the opening measure of Debussy's *Clair de Lune* would be much harder to follow. There is a definite rhythm for this piece, but the melody plays with it freely. The fact that, listening to the passage for the first time, one cannot easily find pulse beats to tap to does not mean that rhythm is absent. It is present, but buried; and it affects the temporal design of the melody in very much the same way as a wave in the sea affects the ripples which twist and run on its surface.

The modern concert dance is seldom a rigidly fixed form, though it is undeniably rhythmical. Within a single short passage of movement, a dancer may have to change the time of his feet and body in half a dozen different ways. He may have to beat out one rhythm with his feet and swing his body or arms to an entirely different rhythm, and then after a few measures change to still another design. His movements may seem to be almost without pattern and scarcely related at all to the music which prompts his actions; but a trained observer is able

to see the design, and the layman, though unable to catch
the underlying rhythm with his mind, feels the pulse beats
through his senses.

The same kind of relationships between fundamental

HIDDEN RHYTHM

The opening measures of Debussy's *Clair de Lune*. (Copyright 1905.
Permission granted by Jean Jobert, Paris, and Elkan-Vogel Co., Philadelphia.)

pulsation and surface movement occurs in the best of stage pantomime. Though buried, the basic rhythms are there, and they constitute a potent force in the creation of emotion.

SPACE DANCING IN ACTING

The two things to be considered in connection with the second element of dancing, space, are the form of movement and the extent of it. They both affect acting. The fundamental movements of the dance and of dramatic pantomime are, of course, the same—walking, running, leaping, reaching, lifting, rising, sitting, lying, struggling. But far too often the dancer manages the movements better than the actor, simply because the actor's body is untrained. The capable actor learns, like the dancer, the values of strong co-ordinated movements carried through to completion, balance, and preparedness for change, for he realizes that these are an essential part of his expressive equipment. Effective dramatic pantomime, he knows, is movement which, while it holds faithfully to the requirements of true characterization, is so filled with strong, free, rhythmical action that it looks every moment as if it would break out into pure dance.

In an effort to get "good form" in pantomime, many teachers of acting have attempted to set down rules of gesture. Similar rules were once made for the dancer. But both dancer and actor realize that no rules of the kind indicated are very helpful. So much depends on the demands of character and situation, and on the personality of the performer himself, that rules of design are more likely to be a hindrance than an aid. But one thing dancer and actor must strive for constantly, *to use the space about them*. There cannot be any breadth of expressiveness when the feet, the body, are rooted in one spot. The dancer and the dancer-actor must possess space. And they must possess it *all*. They take it and make it theirs by filling it with action; and when they cannot actually extend their bodies through every part of it, they show by posture and suggestive gesture that implicitly they are using the rest of the space. Even in the quietest, most reflective moments, when the performer is seated in a chair, his spirit, his muscles, reach out to the farthest limits of the spectator's vision, and fill it with the feeling of stirring forces. The limits of the space which must thus be filled with motion may be the walls of a little sharecropper's shack or the dome of stars above a prairie.

FORCE DANCING IN ACTING

There cannot rightly be any sense of space possession unless the performer exerts himself and continues to exert himself all the time he is in sight of the spectator. The great secret of unbroken movement for the actor lies in sustaining in his body a *condition of aliveness*. This in dancing is called "dynamism." It means behavior in which the muscles never appear flabby; there is always some tension. Still or in motion, the body is energized, ready for action.

Much has been said about the value of "relaxation" in acting, and we do not wish here to unsay any of it. It is absolutely necessary for the player to be able at will to reduce tension in his muscles. He cannot act at all if he walks out before the spectator in a stiffened condition with all his muscles tight. When he is too tense, he is un-

DRAWN DOWN BY THE FORCE OF GRAVITY

prepared. He is unable to change in accordance with the shifting requirements of the scene. There must be an ebb as well as a flow. But ebb never means collapse. Even in situations which call for the loosening of tension, the spectator should be able to observe some tone in the actor's body—preparedness for change. Often the word "rest," with respect to a stage character's actions, does have an absolute meaning. But for the actor, as an actor, "rest" can never be more than comparative. It is to be regretted that many players of the naturalistic school do not appreciate this difference.

Like the other dance factors, time and space, force has two aspects: gross strength, and intensity. The dancer and the dancer-actor differentiate carefully between them. When a performer employs gross strength, he may lift a heavy object, hurl his opponent across the room, or leap a great distance into the air. When the force of his action is marked by intensity, he may use a very little gesture. A mere touch may be filled with such intensity that the spectator will cry aloud.

Having discussed at some length the three factors of the dance, and considered their relationship to the stimulative and expressive technique of the actor, we are ready to explore the problem of interpretation.

TWO PRIMARY INFLUENCES
ON HUMAN BEHAVIOR

There are two primary influences on human behavior. One is biology; the other, society. The first is concerned with the physical welfare of man as an individual—his nutrition, growth, rest, reproduction, general bodily comfort in relation to his environment. Rooted in primitive urges, it is expressed in gross, often violent movements, such as running, leaping, struggling, chasing, fleeing. The social influence is concerned with man's adjustment to other men; and it is manifest chiefly in restraints imposed upon the primitive movements just mentioned. Social expediency, "civilization," demands control.

Among the most potent of the natural forces with which biology must contend is gravity. Out of man's struggle with this force spring many of his fundamental actions. Gravity is a friend; but it is also an enemy, for the human organism must always strive against its oppressive downward pull. When a man is young and strong, full of the essence of life, he stands erect. When old, sick, weary, he succumbs to the pull of gravity and unites himself with the earth. If he cannot again summon strength to push against the force that draws him downward, he dies and is buried. Among the most basic of human feelings is the yearning to be light, free of the earth, to fly. That is why savages leap high into the air, run and dance. That is why Heaven, the symbol of life, is conceived as above us, and Hell, the abode of death, as below.

There are also pleasant, beneficial objects to be approached and harmful objects to be avoided for the biological good of the organism. So, along with rising and sinking, basic large action includes movements toward or away from things. A man moves toward food or a fair woman. He departs from a dangerous animal or another man with a weapon.

A third set of fundamental motions is involved in caring for, building up, "good" objects, and destroying "bad" ones. A mother nourishes her child, a man kills his enemy. To these actions are related the secondary movements of fondling and struggling, for fondling is implicit nurture, and struggling expresses the desire to destroy.

In these three sets of large movements—rising, sinking; approaching, avoiding; nurturing, destroying—we have, perhaps, the most important raw material for dramatic dance pantomime. The six movements are all directly expressive of basically biological urges, primitive action. Over against them there are the restraints imposed by social custom. Every person who would live with other human beings must consider, besides his own, the primary comforts of his neighbors; and so, of course, in accordance with certain regulations on conduct evolved by the majority after long experience, he learns to curb the too free expression of his natural impulses. If, however, the blood of life runs rich in his arteries, he will often find it hard to keep the urges under. Then there is struggle. Effective dance acting manifests a fine balance between the forces of biology and society.

In the pantomimic portrayal of a primitive man the basic urges expressed in large movements will be more evident. In the portrayal of a sophisticated character the fundamental movements will be less immediately manifest. But, explicit or implicit, they should be there. When Hamlet, in court, replies softly to the evil insinuations of his uncle, the spectator should sense that the prince is trembling with a scarcely controllable desire to leap upon the king and beat him into insensibility. When Hester and Christina in *The Silver Cord* watch their jealous mother-in-law seduce the affections of her sons, the audience should feel beneath the surface of their courteous behavior the urge to tear the hair of the older woman and scratch her eyes out. The impulses of the savage are there, ready at any moment to break out. If they finally do break out, in

RISING AGAINST THE FORCE OF GRAVITY

YIELDING TO THE FORCE OF GRAVITY

DRAWN TO A DESIRABLE, BENEFICIAL OBJECT

The object compelling the movement may be food, a child, or a person
offering help.

REPELLED BY AN UNDESIRABLE OBJECT

The object is something repugnant or harmful.

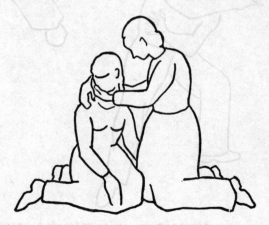

YIELDING TO THE IMPULSE TO NURTURE, BUILD UP

YIELDING TO THE IMPULSE TO DESTROY

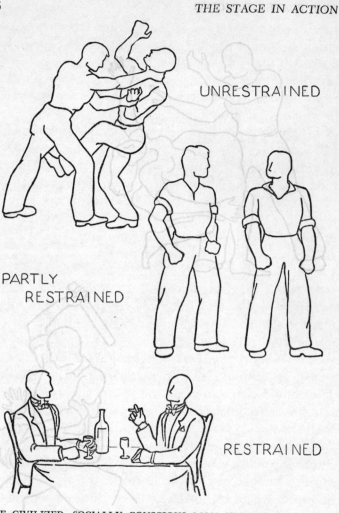

UNRESTRAINED

PARTLY
RESTRAINED

RESTRAINED

**THE CIVILIZED, SOCIALLY CONSCIOUS MAN IS FUNDAMENTALLY
A SAVAGE**

He possesses the same strong impulses as the primitive man, but he
restrains them.

spite of all the restraints of "civilization," the action is exciting. Scenes in which apparently well-bred persons lose control of their actions and begin to move as they feel are invariably dramatic, for we are all savages under our skin. A good example is the scene in *The House of Connelly* in which Will, losing patience with the ceaseless effort of his family to maintain the respectability of the Connelly name in the face of moral and economic bankruptcy, suddenly cries out and hurls his body about the room against the ghosts which torment him. An even better example, because it is more direct, is the scene in the garden, on the night of the party, when Will comes upon Uncle Bob forcing his attention on the girl Patsy, and strikes the old man into the dirt.

The whole episode, including the action before and after Will's discovery and loss of temper, makes strong demands on all three of the fundamental types of movement described above. For the clear translation of the relationships between Will, Uncle Bob, and Patsy in visual symbols there must be explicit movements toward and away from the objects of their desire or aversion. There must be the caresses of love and the struggling action indicative of hatred and the wish to destroy. When Will saw the old man on the ground, and realized in what a cowardly way he himself had acted, he would probably sit down, and his whole body would sink toward the same dirt to which he had struck his uncle. But the death pull of gravity would be broken by the comforting words and the warm body of Patsy beside him. Under her spell Will's head and shoulders would gradually lift, and finally he would rise straight up in a sort of ecstatic defiance of the downward force. As the girl regenerates in Will the surge of life, the attitude of his body must show it.

The more richly emotional is the play, the more it depends for its projection on the fine design of strong movement. One has only to recall the plays of Shakespeare and Ibsen, and such modern favorites as *Anna Christie, They Knew What They Wanted, What Price Glory,* and *Street Scene,* to realize how important to them is the kind of action here described. Even in such comparatively "quiet" compositions as Eugene O'Neill's *Beyond the Horizon* the basic forces stir. In the pantomimic interpretation of such a play there might not be any violent approaches and retreats, risings and sinkings, buildings-up and tearings-down, but little movements would suggest the underlying urges to engage in these actions. *Beyond the Horizon* is, in one sense, a highly "civilized" play, and many of the primitive hungers are sublimated into desires equally urgent but less immediate. The title of the play indicates the principal sublimation. But the basic action patterns are still fundamental to the interpretation.

Plays dealing with simple characters often seem more exciting than the more sophisticated dramas. It is significant that most of the plays which have received the Pulitzer award in this country have been down-to-earth pieces. One strong reason for the dramatic effects produced by the primitive type of action is the comparatively uninhibited movement. In the play of more "civilized" people, the aboriginal impulses are covered with layers of social taboo. The problem of the actor and the director in interpreting the sophisticated scene is therefore greater,

because when they deal with it they often have to create
by implication *images* of the primitive movements.

Images of these movements are made through devices
of indirect statement. The *urge* for the large movement is
the most important thing to be revealed, and this can be
done in several different ways: by small movements of
the body, feet, hands, or head, suggestive of force breaking from under the lid of inhibition; by active tones of
the voice; and, by the method of implied opposites, by
visual hints of the restraining power. A soldier, about to
be shot against the wall, stands unnaturally straight. The
pose is indicative of a determination to face death proudly.
The exaggeration reveals the fact that soldier's "front"
costs effort, and suggests, therefore, that beneath that
civilized exterior there is a strong primitive impulse to
run.

Even the vivid recounting on the stage of large movements—basic, space-taking actions—which have occurred
off stage, or before the play began, often helps to give
the little movements actually presented significance which
would otherwise be missed. The spectator, by imagination, feels through the "civilized" forms back to the powerful first impulses. The effect produced by the description
is immeasurably stronger if the original action takes place
not off stage but on, and the spectator, listening to the
recital, recalls the definite shapes.

SENSUOUS VALUES OF
LARGE-MOVEMENT DESIGN

There is another reason, besides the need for expressive action, why large-movement design in dance acting is commonly more effective than small movement. That is the need for forceful sensuous appeal.

In *Principles of Physical Education*, Jesse F. Williams shows how the nerve centers of the human body are connected with the various types of muscles, and how those that control the muscles of the trunk are older and tougher, and have by nature more endurance, than those controlling the muscles of the extremities. This condition exists because, as we have already noted, the early men and women from whom we are descended had to be equipped for the large, strong movements of jumping, swinging, chasing, and fleeing. These movements, even if we do not now engage in them, are still natural to us; and if we deny ourselves too completely the experience of them, or movements equivalent to them, we are likely to feel the lack. "Physical strength, endurance, power will always be needed as a basis for the operation of the nervous system." [4] City-bred people who as children never had an adequate opportunity to exercise their fundamental muscles are very likely to suffer from nervous disorders. There is everywhere a great desire to sense free action in one's own body, or to feel it out in others. Evidence for the statement can be found in the tremendous volume of sports goods sold annually and the number of people who attend football, baseball, basketball and hockey games, tennis and boxing matches, and races of every kind.

In the theatre, also, men and women find a vicarious pleasure in sensuously feeling out the large, free, rhythmical movements of trained actors in performance. In these brief experiences they find some compensation for those long hours of discomfort through which their starved muscles and minds are held tight by the hard bands of daily life in offices and apartments. The more people become affected by their closed-in activities, the more they tend to seek out for themselves attractive patterns of free movement to which they can periodically become attached—patterns with concentrated power of effect, designed by artists who understand the spectators' hunger and can satisfy it. In the theatre, large, rhythmical movements tend not only to stimulate and express, but also to refresh.

THE DANCER-ACTOR'S TRAINING:
SENSORY ALIVENESS

The spectator in the theatre is equipped to respond, not with his senses and his mind severally, but with all working together as a unit, and he finds the richest satisfaction when the performance on the stage evokes in him this kind of whole response. Man thinks and acts with his mind and all his organs, and he likes to react in the same way. But of course there cannot be any singleness of response without singleness of stimulation. The brain, the voice, and all the members of the dancer-actor's body must speak together. Only so will the performance be richly, fully evocative. The dancer-actor cannot produce fully stimulative action until he has trained himself to use effectively every part of his bodily equipment.

First he must manifest the liveness of all his sensory apparatus. He must show clearly his sensuous awareness of all the stimulating influences which bear on situation and action. The player gives particular attention to those sensory parts which are related to seeing, hearing, and touching, for it is through these channels that he draws most of the nutriment for his dramatic responses. These parts include the eyes, the ears, the fingers and the palms of hands, the soles of the feet, the skin.

Indications of awareness through these several agents are expressive each in its own peculiar way. Few players exploit thoroughly the dramatic possibilities latent in them. These remarks apply with special force to the use of two of the sensory parts, the eyes and the palms of the hands. The eyes, particularly of young actors, seldom give adequate recognition to other human presences on the stage. And reactions, when properly managed, can be extremely expressive. The manner in which a person holds a coin, or a woman places her hand on a man's head, may say more about character and situation than pages of dialogue.

THE DANCER-ACTOR'S TRAINING:
USING EVERY MEMBER
OF THE BODY

In the second place, the dancer-actor must understand the expressive function of every member of his body and have it under complete control.

The Torso. The most important member of the panto-mimic family is the central one. In the torso, or trunk, first are contained the vital organs (the stomach, the heart, the lungs, the bowels, etc.) which are intimately associated with the feeling of emotion, and consequently, with the impulses of the body to move. In the torso, second, are the primary muscles for action, those of the waist, back, neck, shoulders, and hips.

Fundamentally, the most expressive movements of the human body are those related in one way or another to positive and negative attractability, that is, appetencies for and aversions to objects. A love of, a pleasing interest in, or a desire for, an object normally includes an urge to approach that object. A fear of, or a disinterest in, the object naturally creates an impulse to avoid it.* Hatred of an object often brings into existence both the positive and the negative impulses—to approach the object (in order) to cast it aside.

The two basic types of reaction described here are ex-

* Broadly speaking, the first four types of actions described on pages 68–69 may be related to the positive and negative attraction indicated here.

pressed first of all, actually or implicitly, in a forward or backward reaching, or a turning, of the torso. In the primitive body, in the child's for instance, this movement of the trunk may be observed clearly. In the "cultivated"

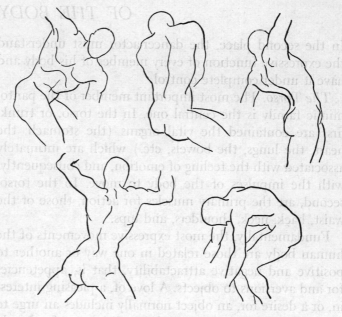

THE TORSO

The torso, where the toughest, strongest muscles of the body are located, is the control center for all large movement.

body, however, the movement of the vital central portion is likely to be inhibited, and the impulses representing positive and negative responses to objects are made manifest in the action of the secondary agents—the legs, the arms, and the head. In the aged body the torso re-

mains inexpressive, except in a passive way, because the
joints of the backbone have become stiffened. One of the
things which characterize an elderly person is his inability
under ordinary circumstances effectively to demonstrate
his fundamental impulses with the central part of his
body. In moments of violent attraction and repulsion,

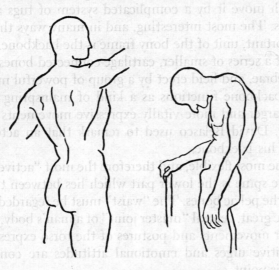

THE TORSO IN YOUTH AND AGE

however, the primary movements are usually revealed
even in the aged body.

The character of the forward and backward urges of
the torso is influenced, of course, not only by instinctive,
but also by acquired, states of mind—grief, despair, hu-
mility, indecision, joy, awe. If the primitive emotions are
manifested through action, the acquired emotions are
usually manifested through posture. Posture expresses also

simple physical states—strength, weakness, exhaustion.

Special attention may be called to the pantomimic value of the back and waist. Anatomically the human body is formed, as we know, of two factors: a bony supporting frame, which is not rigid, but is hinged in numerous places; and muscles which are hung on that frame, and which move it by a complicated system of tugs and releases. The most interesting, and in many ways the most important, unit of the bony frame is the backbone. Made up of a series of smaller, cartilage-connected bones called vertebrae, and held erect by a group of powerful muscles, the backbone functions as a kind of mainspring for all the larger and more vitally expressive movements of the body. David Belasco used to remark that an actor acts with his backbone.

The most flexible, and therefore the most "active," part of the spine is the lower part which lies between the ribs and the pelvic bones. The "waist" must be regarded, then, as the great, central "master joint" of a man's body. Those larger movements and postures of the torso expressive of primitive urges and emotional attitudes are controlled at this point.

The Legs. The legs are expressive chiefly as the carrying agents for the body. Moving backward and forward in action patterns we call "steps," they extend and accentuate the manifestations, first noted in the torso, of a man's desire to make or break contacts with objects. Through the manner of their movement they also show the state of mind which conditions or characterizes this desire. The actions of the feet indicate more clearly, perhaps, than those of any other part of the body (with the possible exception of the face) a man's happiness, sor-

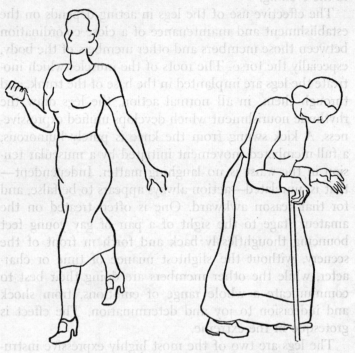

THE MOVEMENT OF THE FEET IS DRAMATIC

The manner of a person's walking reveals his character, age, and physical and emotional condition.

row, indecision, embarrassment, determination, pride, or joy of living.

The actions of the feet show unmistakably also the physical condition of the man. Consider the contrast between the manner of his walk when he goes to his shop or his office in the morning and the manner when he returns in the evening.

The effective use of the legs in acting depends on the establishment and maintenance of a close co-ordination between those members and other members of the body, especially the torso. The roots of the muscles which motivate the legs are implanted in the base of the trunk, and through them, in all normal action, the legs draw the rhythmic nourishment which develops unified expressiveness. A kick swung from the knee is purely humorous; a full-membered movement initiated by a muscular tension in the waist is no laughing matter. Independent— that is, unrelated—action always appears to be false, and for that reason awkward. One is often treated on the amateur stage to the sight of a pair of gay young feet bouncing thoughtlessly back and forth in front of the scenery, without the slightest nuance of time or character, while the other members are doing their best to communicate a whole range of emotions, from shock and indecision to joy and determination. The effect is grotesque in the extreme.

The legs are two of the most highly expressive instruments of the human body. It is to be regretted that they are so frequently used on the stage only for ornament.

The Arms. The arms, in common with the torso and the legs, are expressive first of attractability, the impulse of a man to make or to break contact with an object. When the torso leans forward, and the legs carry forward, the arms reach forward to touch, to grasp, to draw in the object. When the torso leans or turns away, and the legs

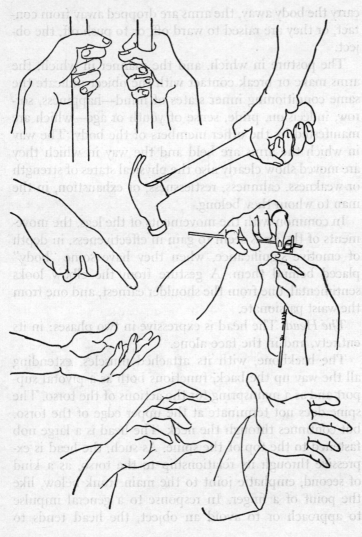

HANDS

Hands feel, grasp, work. Sometimes also they point out, communicate thought. Few actors use their hands as effectively as they might.

carry the body away, the arms are dropped away from contact, or they are raised to ward off, or to push off, the object.

The posture in which, and the manner in which, the arms make or break contact with the object indicate the same conditioning inner states of mind—happiness, sorrow, indecision, pride, sense of youth or age—which are manifested by the other members of the body. The way in which the arms are held and the way in which they are moved show clearly also the physical states of strength or weakness, calmness, restlessness, or exhaustion, in the man to whom they belong.

In common with the movements of the legs, the movements of the arms seem to gain in effectiveness, in depth of emotive significance, when they have some "body" placed behind them. A gesture from the elbow looks sentimental, one from the shoulder earnest, and one from the waist passionate.

The Head. The head is expressive in two phases: in its entirety, and in the face alone.

The backbone, with its attached muscles, extending all the way up the back, functions both as a pivotal support and as a mainspring for the actions of the torso. The spine does not terminate at the upper edge of the torso, but continues through the neck. The head is a large nob fastened to the top of the spine. As such, the head is expressive through its relationship to the torso, as a kind of second, emphatic joint to the main trunk below, like the point of a finger. In response to a general impulse to approach or to avoid an object, the head tends to turn and reach toward or away from the object in the same direction as the torso, but farther.

Physical and mental states are reflected clearly in the posture of the head. A man betrays his attitude toward himself in the way he holds the topmost member of his body. When the head is held erect, self-esteem is manifested; when it is dropped, the indications of pride are removed. But the feelings which prompt the assumption of this posture come from below. A bowed head does not mean much unless the torso is also bowed. The reverse is likewise true. When spirit comes into a man bent with the thought of his own worthlessness, breath enters his lungs, his waist muscles tighten, his chest expands; his head does not rise first unless it is to observe the source of promised inspiration—that is, to offer a channel through eyes and ears for the inflowing. When spirit comes, it affects the central sections of the body first.

A realization of the importance of the posture of the head in indicating a man's estimation of himself should emphasize the value of an erect carriage for all dominating characters on the stage. A hero or a heroine with slumped head and shoulders loses spirit. One cannot in this posture give the impression of lungs filled with "vital air."

But the chief expressive values of the head lie in the face. The face is the focal and emphatic center of physical and mental expression. After observing the more general posture and action of the body as a whole, one looks to the face for a sharpening of the impression. The face is man's most important reception center. There are senses here for sight, hearing, smell, taste, and (to a certain extent) touch. The expressiveness of the face is largely concerned with indications of sense activity. That is, the organs of sight, smell, and hearing are indicative of a state of mind in a passive way only. The mouth, which forms speech, is pre-eminently the active member of the family of features.

The Body as a Whole. The visible, active body is expressive in a number of ways. Through forward and backward movement, a reaching toward or away, the body manifests, as we have observed, a man's general urge to make or to break contact with objects. The action which signifies the urge may be actual or implied. When the action is to be implied on the stage, perceptible symbols of the action—a visible tension, a parallel movement in other members, a significant tone of voice—must, of course, be provided. *A spectator can never read an actor's impulse except through some outward indication of its existence.*

Man is a sensuous being. He enjoys many contacts. But he fears some. He is always hungry, physically, intellectually, emotionally. He works, he plays, he feeds himself, he travels, he communicates with other people—to satisfy these hungers. Satisfaction comes through contact. A man's life is filled with a continuous stream of impulses to approach or to avoid things. Some of these things lie in the visible world; some of them lie wholly within the mind. Drama deals only with *perceptible* contacts; yet many of a man's contacts, in his day-by-day existence, are purely inward, unrecognizable by other people because not outwardly made evident. This "daily" behavior must

be adapted, then, when it is brought to the theatre. When
the inward action of a character is to be depicted on the
stage, it becomes the duty of the playwright, of the actors
and the other artists of the stage, to place before the audience clearly visible and audible symbols, people and objects with seeable and hearable qualities, which may represent by implication those things that the inner senses
of the character to be portrayed apperceive (form contact with); and then it is the business of the player who
personates the character to translate into an outward
pantomimic and vocal form the image of the inner response. The audience, perceiving the outward reaction
to the outward symbol, senses imaginatively the inward contact with the inward object. Hamlet's reactions
to the dark objects of his mind, for instance, are revealed in his responses to those outward symbols represented by the words and actions of Polonius and Ophelia,
by the throne, the grave, and other figures in the play.

The four pantomimic agents, the torso, the legs, the
arms, and the head, employed by the actor to communicate his message to the spectator, have been considered
separately in these pages, not in order to emphasize any
independently expressive qualities in each, but to show
how much each member has to contribute to the expressive whole. The larger organism of the body, made up of
all the physical members, plus the voice, should sit, should
talk, work, play, should seem happy, discouraged, weary,
or strong, should sense the presence of objects, be at-
tracted or repulsed, as a single instrument. The movements of the torso, the legs, the arms, the head, and the
features of the face should be synchronized absolutely,

and the summation of the pantomimic body fitted carefully to the time and tone of the voice for the purpose of producing one dramatic effect.

THE DANCER-ACTOR'S TRAINING:
CONTROL

The third point in the training of the dancer-actor is his development of control. He must train himself by exercise, like the concert dancer, to be strong, flexible, and prepared, capable of performing every kind of movement, large or small, and ready to do it instantly on command. He must prepare himself also to make all movements neatly and gracefully—that is, without any apparent waste of energy. The moment-by-moment supply of that effort which an audience is willing to expend in its attention to a performer's actions is limited. When the action observed is awkward and indirect and fails to accomplish its objective without fumbling, the attention of the spectator is distracted. Through the sensations derived from "feeling-into" (discussed in the closing chapter of the book), every observer has a tendency to suffer the same kind of bodily discomfort as that experienced on the stage by the actor who is *inefficient* or *incomplete* in his physical movements. Herbert Spencer defines grace as "motion that is effected with economy of force."

The price of a set of strong, live, dependable muscles is, of course, constant exercise. Sports provide excellent

THE BODY OF THE ATHLETE
The athlete, like the modern dancer, uses his whole body, with the center of power and control in the torso.

training, but they are not enough. Sport exercises should
be supplemented by special setting-up exercises designed
to strengthen and quicken those particular parts of the
player's body which have a tendency to become flabby—
the back, perhaps, or the neck or hips. The kinds of exercises which are employed to build up the bodies of concert dancers are especially useful for this purpose.

The development of control means not only training
the body to perform single movements together in expressive design. Through a study of music, the dancer-actor
must build up a ready sense of rhythm, changing tempo,
volume, and force. He must master the technique of subordination and accent, and he must understand fully the
values of phrasing. Phrasing means the grouping together
of several elements, and the following of them by a momentary pause—like a catch for breath in singing—before
the beginning of the next series. Effective pantomime
shows periodic action, periodic rest. One has only to glance
at the crude, unbroken movement in an old film play like
The Great Train Robbery, and then to compare with it
the beautifully punctuated action of a recent picture like
The Citadel, or *Gone with the Wind*, to realize the
importance of good phrasing.

A sense for good phrasing, like that for rhythm, can be
sharpened by the study of musical forms. From these
one will learn that phrases may be regular, as with Mozart, or quite free and irregular, like those in a composition by Stravinsky. The technique of phrasing will be
discussed at greater length in another chapter.

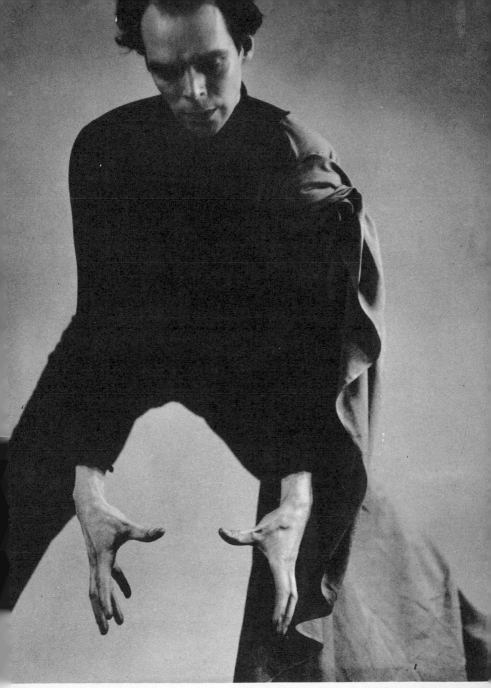

THE DANCER'S CONTROL OF HIS BODY

The dancer's use of his hands: Charles Weidman in *Candide*.

Thomas Bouchard

THE DANCER'S CONTROL OF HER BODY

The use of the whole body in movement: Hanya Holm in *Trend*.

CREATIVENESS

If all the plays an actor is called upon to interpret were of the same formal design, such as Greek tragedies, the dancer-actor could develop one pantomimic technique and stick to it. But the pieces in which he appears today are as varied as the moods of the authors who write them. In a single season the actor may perform in a realistic folk play like *Sun-up,* a smart comedy like *Hay Fever,* a poetic play like *Winterset,* an expressionistic piece like *The Adding Machine,* and an operetta like *Patience.* Clearly, therefore, his pantomime technique cannot be fixed. His dance acting must be free and flexible, adaptable to every new dramatic situation which arises.

The necessity for mobility in pantomime style would seem to be obvious; yet it is constantly ignored by professonals and amateurs alike. For some reason the importance of flexibility in vocal delivery is more quickly recognized than the need for flexibility in physical action. Many players turning to *Romeo and Juliet* from *Beyond the Horizon,* say, readily catch the swing of the verse dialogue, without altering the prose movement of their feet. And they do not seem to be aware of their half-inexpressiveness. The visual side of their technique is fixed. They have early acquired the use of certain pantomimic devices, and because these have proved themselves to be effective in a number of situations, the dependence on them has become habitual.

The actor can be sure that his dance pantomime is fresh and fully expressive only if he has firmly resolved to do no "leaning"—that is, if he treats the interpretation of each play as a fresh problem, not to be solved by the use of other men's methods and his own past technique.

Chapter Four

THE PLAYER
SINGING

THE SPOKEN WORD:
ARTICULATED SOUNDS AND TONE

Speech is an art—at once the most familiar, the most extraordinary, and the least understood of all the arts. Extremely complex, its psychology and techniques are wholly mastered by few. Yet those who daily study the ways of speech and exploit it for the projection of emotion and thought number more than the workers in all other fields combined. One reason why the inner form of speech is so elusive is that, far ahead of those arts which deal solely with line, color, or musical sound, it is a synthesis of factors drawn from every walk of human experience. Intimately related to each of the senses, in both static and dynamic states, its expressive range extends all the way from the purely descriptive, or indicative, to the abstract. The art of speech touches life at every point of its progress.

For the lingual scientist, speech is primarily a system of articulated vowel and consonant sounds, affected by

inflectional patterns characteristic of a racial or sectional
group of people. For the artist, however, it is something
more. Beside the articulative elements there is another,
musical tone. The laws which govern the standard composition of words are, for each language, set and unalter-
able. With regard to vowel and consonant parts, the
words "house," "girl," "love," and "lonesome" can be
made in only one way. But with regard to the tonal
changes which may be made around these words, there
are practically no limits. In speaking them one may raise
his voice, lower it, extend it, shorten it, harden it, soften
it, play upon it in a hundred different ways.

The full value of the tonal element is rarely appreciated.
Yet it is a fact that without tone words are barren of
expression. Let one take, for example, the word YES, and
ask what, in plain terms, the word suggests. Then let one
intone the word. Affected by changes in quality and inflection, it may mean different things. It may give certain assurance or indicate doubt, it may ask a question,
or express irritation or a great weariness. There is a mis-
chievous YES, an inviting YES, an angry YES, a YES which
implies a command, a YES which means no. Now, let one
put the word into a sentence like the following and note
the many different meanings which alterations in tone
cause in the line as a whole: *Yes, I shall remember you
always.*

There are innumerable stories of actors who have been
able to affect their hearers practically without "words" at
all. Madame Modjeska once brought tears to the eyes of
an English audience by reciting with feeling the multipli-
cation table in Polish. An accomplished friend of the

Italian tragedian, Ernesto Rossi, swept the emotions of a table full of companions by vocally interpreting a menu. An able comedian convulsed a party of friends by reading a list of names and numbers from a telephone directory. The conclusion to which we are brought, after hearing these and other such stories, is that bare words in a line of speech are like the bones of a skeleton. They have form, but no personality. The bones must be covered with warm flesh, and there must be breath and pulse, before there is life. The tonal music of the speaker expresses, far more than his vowel and consonant sounds ever can, his character, his general circumstances, and his changing reactions to environment.

THE SINGER IN THE ACTOR

What we call "voice" is produced by a marvelously complex instrument consisting of reedlike membranes in a bony box, three resonating chambers, a tongue-and-lip-controlled outlet, and bellows, all subject to sensitive adjustment by more than thirty muscles. With training, the instrument can make a series of notes extending over two octaves with, at will, many changes of quality. Tonal changes include timbre and other factors, affected to an infinite extent by variations in pitch, time, and force. The human speech apparatus is the most flexible musical instrument in the world; and every tonal resource connected with it is used in speaking.

The stimulative and expressive values of pure musical

tone produced by a mechanical instrument, and especially
the human voice, are readily acknowledged by everyone.
What is not so quickly recognized is the value of the same
kind of tonal play when it appears as a component of
free speech. "Often," says the Jewish poet, Pérez, "the
song is higher than the spoken word, because often one
can express in music thoughts that words can never tell."
But why must that eloquence beyond words be divorced
from words? Why may not the magical melody sound
through them, and so affect the hearer on the fundamental plane of his understanding? It will be our purpose
in this chapter to show that music and verbal communication are united.

VOCAL TONE
AND ITS PROPERTIES

The basic element in musical effect lies, as already observed, in tone; and tone, especially vocal tone, stirs the
listener with a peculiar power because it is intimately
connected with every part of man's conscious life. The
primary function of the ear is to keep the human organism adjusted to its environment. Dr. James L. Mursell says in *The Psychology of Music*: "The neural connections of the ear are of special and direct importance
in giving the sense of balance, of up and down, of direction, upon which controlled bodily movement depends.
And thus music is an art which employs a medium—aural

experience—associated with unique intimacy with our feeling of bodily movement and control." Tone acts directly upon the neural mechanisms, arousing in the listener a wide range of feelings with respect to his surroundings. High, intense tones tend to produce a feeling of alarm, danger, general excitement, whereas low, soft tones are calming, reassuring, may even put one to sleep. Says Dr. Mursell: "Aural experience is uniquely associated with the instinctive and emotional reactions throughout animal life. It is the great conveyor of warnings, incitements, cajoleries, and challenges. And we as human beings unquestionably share this inheritance." [1]

Discussing the effects of music in *Art as Experience*, John Dewey makes the same observations regarding the physical, emotional influence of tone. "Sound," he says, "is the conveyor of what impends, of what is happening as an indication of what is likely to happen. It is fraught much more than vision with the sense of issues." [2] Sound, idealized in musical tone, is the most direct agent for the feelings of expectancy and fulfillment, the sense of adjustment to one's surroundings.

As already intimated, the most powerfully stirring tones are those produced by the human vocal instrument. And the reason for this is something even more profound than just the qualities of the physical tone itself. Human tone, unlike the violin or the organ tone, carries at its core the sound of the moving body. The fundamental agent in the transmitting apparatus is the diaphragm. This mysterious, as yet little understood member of the body plays a central part in man's experience, quite aside from its obvious function as a unit in the breathing apparatus.

VOCAL TONE IS THE SOUND OF AN ACTIVE BODY

The movement of tone is based on the overt or implicit movement of
the physical body.

"The diaphragm and its associates, both nervous and muscular, reach into the deepest recesses of the individual," says Mabel Todd in *The Thinking Body*. The diaphragm "is tied up with every living function, from the psychic to the structural, and within its nervous mechanism sends out ramifications to the remotest points of the sphere of living." [3] The listener senses in the changing tones of another man's words the changing activity of his diaphragm, and, through that, feels deep into the general stir of all the speaker's nervous and muscular members. One does not need to look at a man to tell whether he is standing or reclined, whether he is still, moving slowly or rapidly, whether he is relaxed or tense in his attitude, smiling or trembling with rage, fear, or hatred. Every bodily state casts its reflection aurally in the tone of speech.

Some of the observations which have been made in these pages regarding the properties of the human voice apply to unmusical as well as musical speech. But to appreciate the stimulating and expressive effects at their most powerful point one must seek for them on the level of tone. Noisy speech is definitely limited in effective values. For one thing, its expressive range is extremely narrow, and for another it tends so strongly to repel the ear of the listener that sensitive hearing is made impossible. "It causes fatigue, increases tension, lowers the levels of performance in almost all types of mental and physical work, and in general militates against efficient function." [4] Tone, however, as already noted, works upon the listener in a directly contrary way. It stimulates the organic processes, reduces fatigue, invites attention.

Dramatic speech may be said, then, to reach the level

of true eloquence only when it is akin to music, when it "sings." In tone, quivering with sensuous life and active with melody and rhythm, may lie all the essences of man's dynamic character—his desires, his dreams, his ceaseless efforts to adjust his restless being to the presences which surround him.

TONE DESCRIBES, GIVES OUTWARD SENSE OF OBJECTS

The communicative values of tone produced by the human instrument lie broadly in two fields, sensuous and dynamic. The effective rendering of descriptive and contemplative passages leans heavily on the first. Speech designed to reflect the urge to move employs the second. Purely sensuous tone is commonly associated with the impulse to *feel*, dynamic tone with the impulse *to do*. Both types of tone are frequently demanded in the same speech, though the emphasis may be on one or the other.

Let us consider separately the two sets of values, taking first the sensuous. Tone, in general, is found to possess very definite and consistent qualities. Everyone knows tone which is "hard" or "soft," "rough" or "smooth." It may also be "big" or "little," "rich" or "thin." The tactile values which are natural to live tone make vivid to the listener all the qualities of objects "felt" by the speaker, even when descriptive terms are omitted. The speaker's experience of "stone," "pudding," "wind," or "skin" may be communicated quite clearly without an adjective.

Because descriptive tones are remarkably transparent, the sensuous effectiveness is directly dependent on the sensuous attitude of the man speaking. The term "big," uttered without feeling, is thoroughly neutral. Its descriptive force for a particular object becomes apparent, then, only when the speaker himself is conscious of stretch. A figure called "tiny" will not *feel* to the listener to be very different from the one called "large" unless there is a suggestion that the speaker has narrowed his own scope of sensing. Something apprehended to be really "wide" or "high" or "distant" or "deep" is characterized vocally by an extension of sound which indicates directly the perceptual and emotional reach of the observer. Not only the shape but the direction of that reach may be indicated. The human voice tends to go in the direction of the speaker's attention, up or down, in or out. When the object or quality contemplated is apart from the body of the speaker, his voice reaches out toward it. When it is united with him, his voice retires, often turns inward. His tone, when it is attached to himself, commonly reflects his sense of his own posture, being full and "puffy" when he lifts his chest and struts, shrunken when he droops his shoulders in weakness or discouragement.

The dramatically descriptive value of tone play may be clearly demonstrated in two renderings of the following poem, "Subject for a Farce," by Paul Eldridge.

> Night—
> An old woman sitting at the window—
> Dreaming . . .
> Suddenly,
> Softly,

Her name is called—
"Florence—Florence—Florence!"
She shivers—
Rises—
Bends out—
A neighbor's window opens,
A gentle voice whispers—
"All right, dearest—come up—I am alone" . . .
An old woman standing at the window,
Dreaming . . .[5]

Read the poem straight through in an even tone and steady tempo. It is nearly meaningless. Now reread it with tonal changes descriptively suggesting the different objects, postures, and actions indicated. "Night" is not open like the day; it is shut in, and should be rendered that way. The "old woman" is frail and tired, and the tone attached to her should suggest this. "Dreaming" is quiet, detached, unhurried.

Then a change—"suddenly." But the sound which strikes the ear so unexpectedly comes "softly." It is the old woman's name, and she leans a little toward the window to hear it called, outside. She "shivers," "rises," "bends out"—all these actions are descriptively dramatized by the movements of the narrator's voice. The words the old woman hears are addressed eagerly to someone below. There is a slight pause. Then once again the old woman retires, with the aid of tone, back into herself and her dreams.

AN ACTIVE VOICE COMES FROM AN ACTIVE BODY

Valeska Gert in the dance *Revolt*.

Wootten-Moulton

SONG DRAMA

Scenes from *Fire of the Lord*, by Frank Durham, and *Got No Sorrow*, by Caroline Crum, ritualistic folk plays produced by the Carolina Playmakers.

Wootten-Moulton

TONE INDICATES THE
IMPULSE TO MOVE, FEEL OUT, DO

But the tone play which accompanies a dramatic speaker's words does more, as we have said, than describe objects and actions. It suggests intimately the speaker's impulses to move, feel out things, sense through action differences in value, perform certain deeds. Consider the following passage from the second act of Emlyn Williams's play, *A Murder Has Been Arranged*. Maurice Mullins, ne'er-do-well, addresses a friend:

I've studied myself for years, and I've always been interested in my subject. Here are my conclusions. Some men are born good. They grow up to be saints, or heroes, or preachers, or ideal husbands, as the case may be. Maurice Austin Mullins, however, was born bad. Very bad indeed. I like to be very well dressed, to feel very comfortable in a very big car, with the knowledge that if it breaks down, I have seven others just as big to choose from. I like to buy for every woman I like, everything she likes. I like caviare, and I like champagne. Not because I enjoy the stuff, but because it's so damnably, so gloriously, expensive. Anybody can forge a check.... That's where my artist's touch comes in.... The little nobodies forge their checks with a trembling hand and a sidelong eye, in the quiet of their bedrooms; I forge mine in public, with a flourish, as if I were signing a letter bequeathing a thousand pounds to the Girls' Friendly Society.[6]

Mullins leads a vivid life. The color of his thought is lost completely if his speech is rendered in flat tones. The depth of his own "badness," and his mock shame over it, can be sensed by the auditor only when the tone which describes the "good" man is contrasted in pitch—set on a different sensuous level—from that which describes the evil. When Mullins describes his liking for being well dressed, one should be able, listening sensuously to his tone, to feel the pleasure of putting on good clothes. In the same manner, one should be able to feel the luxurious comfort of stretching out in a "very big car," tossing out money for expensive gifts, foods, and drinks. Then when Mullins draws the contrast between the two ways of forging a check, one should be able to sense, physically, the difference between the fearful little movement in hiding and the grand flourish in the open.

TONE REVEALS
INNER SENSES OF THINGS

The examples given so far have been concrete, tone play suggesting the extrinsic qualities of objects, movements, sensations. However, it can be shown that equivalent tonal changes are vital factors in the communication of abstract thoughts, inner senses of things. The following excerpt comes from an early version of Paul Green's *The Enchanted Maze*. Old Dr. Everett, telling his three remaining students that because of decreasing enrollment his course in ethics will be discontinued and that the class is meeting now for the last time, sits in his chair with his hands resting on the desk before him. Smiling a bit wearily, he acknowledges an expression of sympathy from one of the men present.

One of those testing times I just spoke about. I suppose they keep coming to a man as long as he lives, and the biggest one is the last one. (*Looking out at the empty row of seats.*) I can remember twenty-five years ago this room was filled with students of Ethics. (*Nodding to Parker.*) Your father was one of them—also Mr. Carter. I've taught some of the greatest leaders of the state and nation in this very room. Yes, and a great many fine men of the church. Not so many years ago a large number of my students were future ministers. But today you might search this campus over and not find one in the five thousand boys and girls here. The church is no longer important and only the weaker type of intelligence finds satisfaction in its walls. (*Holding up his hand as Pratt leans forward in his seat.*) But don't think that great institution is dead. Rather, it is in a state of—er—suspended animation. It will some day regain its place. (*Sighing.*) But I shall not.

If one disregards the several minor changes in tonal quality called for in this passage, he will note the requirements for four major changes. The first lines start on a note of depression, which must end when to Dr. Everett's mind, to his inward senses, return the faces of all the splendid men and women who were once his pupils. Surely, as he sees them in the seats before him, he will lean a little forward, his tired body will straighten under the feeling of past power, and his voice will rise and strengthen. When, however, the professor remembers the sad state of the church, he will slump again, physically and vocally. But there is another gathering of forces at the point where he defends the reputation of the "great institution," and a final sinking of body and voice when once more he contemplates his own present impotence.

BODY AND VOICE
UNITED IN COMMUNICATION

It is quite possible to conceive of the tonal play indicated for the passage quoted above with no visible movement whatsoever. Professor Everett may sit quite motionless behind the desk, too tired, or perhaps too proud, to show physically the changes in his thoughts and feelings. Yet, beneath the surface of his outward appearance, there will be some tightening, some relaxing of bodily muscles. This inceptive, but invisible, movement, and also the large, free, visible movements which they imply, can all be reflected in the speaker's intonation—and, if he speaks with true expressiveness, they will be. If Professor Everett is really wrought up in his defense of the church, the audience should be able to "see" him rise to his feet, although the actor playing the character does not twitch a single visible muscle.

In a similar way, it is possible to conceive of active readings of the first two selections in the preceding section—the old woman's experience by the window, and Maurice Mullins's description of his favorite behavior—without any visible accompanying movement. The following dynamic lines from Swinburne's "A Song in Time of Order" could also be uttered from a body outwardly still:

> Push hard across the sand,
>   For the salt wind gathers breath;
> Shoulder and wrist and hand,
>   Push hard as the push of death.

But it is impossible to conceive of any of the *moving* lines in these passages being spoken without an inner sense of touching, hearing, seeing, acting on the part of the speaker. Expressively communicative speech is speech which reflects dynamically the overt or implicit movements connected with live experience. And the active element in this kind of speech is tone. Tone is the sound of a pulsing, breathing, sensuously moving body.

The human organism, as we have pointed out, naturally expresses itself as a single unit. Word tones and muscular activity should never, therefore, be viewed as two distinct agents for communication. They belong together. That this fact is recognized, consciously or unconsciously, not only by successful actors and platform speakers, but also by singers and instrumentalists, is demonstrated by the behavior of musicians in the concert hall. Teachers of singers instruct their students to "use the whole body behind the tone." Vocalists who stand flat-footed while they sing are never very inspiring; their songs lack pulse, sensitivity, movement. Pianists and violinists give considerable thought to the impression made by their "presence" on the stage. Orchestral music heard over the radio seldom produces on the listener any effect commensurate with that given in a hall where one may see the musicians and watch their conductor.

Commenting upon this in *Listening to Music*, Douglas Moore says, "there is something of a psychological nature which occurs when music is performed and which no machinery has yet been able to relay. Just what it is, it is impossible to explain scientifically." [7] There are some factors involved which may not be readily explainable, but the chief one seems to me to be quite clear. It is the *visible*, bodily part of the tonal expression which is absent when music is heard only. We can say that there is less for the auditor-spectator to "feel himself into." Musical tone and the bodily performance of it all belong together in the same expression; and the man who listens finds himself stirred most powerfully when he responds with his ear, his eye, his mind, and every organ of his body.

Tone, then—to return to speech—has a communicative function; and it fulfills this function when it makes the listener sense the movement which lies below the surface of those intellectual symbols which we call "words." The whole human organism, we repeat, moves normally as a unit. There are voice tones which are characteristic of each sensation, posture, and action of the body. When these sounds are given expertly by the speaker, the listener feels himself into the inner, basic activity which they signify. Thus the listener gets to the heart of the speaker's thought.

EMOTIVE VALUES
IN MUSICAL TONES

Coeffective with the communicative values of tone are the emotive. To illustrate, take the following phrase: *I love you.* Uttered without vocal color, the sentence is, of course, a mere statement of fact without emotional significance. If prompted only by the mind, but by no feeling, it is an empty frame of words. When the same words are impregnated with tone, however, the sentence becomes rich with meaning. It may declare to the listener an affectionate or a passionate attachment, or it may proclaim an angry denial of any such attachment. The sentence *I love you* may ask a question; it may give a command. It may persuade the person to whom it is addressed to sing a song; to relax quietly in sleep; or it may influence that person to rise hurriedly and leave the room—perhaps in a furious temper. The basically expressive element in every case is the color of the words in the sentence. But changes in the factors of pitch, force, and pace extend or modify the effects of that color. The possible shadings are almost unlimited.

The tonal expressions in speech and the factors which cause them are fundamentally the same as those in any other kind of musical activity. The function of changing patterns in all vocal and instrumental forms, says James Mursell, is to "capture and convey differences in emotional meaning," and he lists some of the leading factors which contribute to varying mood effects. They are:

High and low pitch
Wide and narrow tonal range
Loudness and softness
Orchestral color
Differences in rhythmic patterns
Rising and falling inflection
Finality trends (such as those produced
by dominant pedal points)
Various tonality relationships,
including modulation [8]

Although Dr. Mursell nowhere in this discussion refers to speech design, he could do so without any modification of his primary points, for his statements concerning the emotional effect of patterns and the operating factors obviously fit the art of speech. How just three of the many possible changes, those in pitch, force, and pace, can influence the effective value of the simple sentence given above is suggested in the following outline.

Change in pitch:

I love you (on a high plane). The affection is fanciful.

I love you (on a lower plane). The affection is deeper, less mental, more physical.

Change in force:

I love you (loudly). The affection is forced upon the listener.

I love you (more quietly). The affection is given tentatively; it asks for a response.

Change in pace:

I love you (quickly). The affection is influenced by nervousness, fear, or bitterness.

I love you (more slowly). The affection is assured—even

though the attainment of the object toward which it is directed may, perhaps, seem hopeless.

The closer we get back to primitive speech, the more we are impressed by the fundamental part music plays in the communication of feeling. We see this nowhere more clearly than in the verse forms. "The poetry of the lowlier tribes," says Mackenzie in *The Evolution of Literature*, "depends more upon music than upon words. . . . The lower we go in the scale of civilization the greater is the dependence of verse upon music, partly because primitive man has an acquired power of introspection. It is here that music excels, for it can still express impulses that are too vague for formulation." [9]

The savage uses music to express feelings for which he has as yet no adequate intellectual symbols. When he develops, through civilization after civilization, up to a place where he has at his command so many words that he requires a book with a thousand pages to hold them, he still must depend on music. For there are no mere words which can communicate through consonant and vowel combinations alone the fundamental urges of the human organism. Music springs out of the tissue of life. It is the essence of life. It is, therefore, the best messenger of life's movement.

The expressive range of tonal patterns extends from the simpler, personal emotions to the most highly complicated feelings related to broad sweeps of life. The German philosopher Schopenhauer long ago pointed out that "suitable music played to any scene, action, event, or surrounding seems to disclose to us its most secret

meaning," and this it does, he says, because music, more
than any other form of expression, reflects man's eternal
hungers and his efforts to satisfy them. Schopenhauer's
argument for the connection between music and the
struggle of the human *will* is elaborate and very interesting. Here is one small excerpt:

"The composer reveals the inner nature of the world.
. . . As quick transition from wish to satisfaction, and
from satisfaction to a new wish, is happiness and well-
being, so quick melodies without great deviations are
cheerful. . . . The short intelligible subjects of quick
dance-music seem to speak only of easily attained common pleasure. On the other hand, the *Allegro maestoso*,
in elaborate movements, long passages, and wide deviations, signifies a greater, nobler effort towards a more distant end, and its final attainment. The *Adagio* speaks of
the pain of a great and noble effort which despises all
trifling happiness. But how wonderful is the effect of the
minor and *major!* How astounding that the change of
half a tone, the entrance of a minor third instead of a
major, at once and inevitably forces upon us an anxious
painful feeling, from which again we are just as instan-
taneously delivered by the major. The *Adagio* lengthens in
the minor the expression of the keenest pain, and becomes
even a convulsive wail. . . . The inexhaustibleness of
possible melodies corresponds to the inexhaustibleness of
Nature in difference of individuals, physiognomies, and
courses of life. The transition from one key to an entirely different one, since it altogether breaks the connection with what went before, is like death, for the individual ends in it." [10]

An eminent philosopher of today, John Dewey, has expressed the same thoughts in a more general way: "Music, having sound as its medium, thus necessarily expresses in a concentrated way the shocks and instabilities, the conflicts and resolutions, that are the dramatic changes enacted upon the more enduring background of nature and human life. The tension and the struggle has its gatherings of energy, its discharges, its attacks and defences, its mighty warrings and its peaceful meetings, its resistances and resolutions, and out of these things music weaves its web." [11]

Schopenhauer and Dewey are referring in these passages, of course, to pure music, not musical tone in speech. But, in essence, what they say of music applies also to speech patterns containing the element of song. Both passages are richly suggestive of why musical utterance can evoke in the listener emotions which words without music can never stir. Beginning with the unit phases of effective speech—the word, the phrase—and progressing through the sentence, the sentence group, and the completed passage or scene, one finds at every point the animating influence of musical factors. The basic factor is, of course, tone. But the stimulating and expressive range of tone is limited when other factors are absent. Tone unvaried soon loses its potency, or produces an effect directly contrary to pleasurable experience. Tone varied, but without order, may stimulate, but only in confusion. The tone factor of speech, like the tone factor in pure music, is effectively exploited only when it is patterned in melody, motivated with rhythm, and developed in accordance with principles of accent, contrast, surge, and climax. Design brings out the latent forces by playing tone against the human senses from many sides on many levels; and it puts larger meaning into tone by showing differences and unions between the different elements of expression. Tonal design mirrors the changing, growing movement of the speaker's inward thoughts and feelings.

Below the level of actual song, no form of utterance makes greater demands upon the musical resources of the speaker than does dramatic dialogue. The language of the theatre is sensuous and dynamic; it bubbles out of dancing bodies moved by the deep play and counterplay of passion, by strong changes of sensation, thought, and mood—sometimes quick, sometimes slow, but always active. The emotions which beat beneath the words are touched with fire; so the tonal design which expresses them must be richly varied, widely ranged.

FACTORS IN DESIGN: PITCH

The fundamental factor of tonal power in song acting is quality; and the primary factors for the exploitation of this power through design are pitch, time, and force. Quality, and its relationship to dramatic effect, has already been dealt with at some length, but the other three factors need additional attention.

Some of the values lying in changes of pitch have been noted. Levels of tone help to communicate the speaker's feelings regarding height and depth, and the lift of the spirit with respect to the force of gravity. When the mind and the body dance, there is a tendency for the voice to rise; when the mind and the body sink to rest, or to death, the tone sinks also. High notes are active, low notes more quiet. The rising intervals in a melodic line often suggest effort, strain, whereas falling intervals suggest relaxation. Words on a high pitch level within the natural range of the speaker's voice seem thinner, less voluminous, but

FACTORS IN TONAL DESIGN: PITCH

often brighter, more cheerful. On a lower level they commonly seem richer, more voluminous, but resigned, and, if very low, depressed, melancholy.

Joy, anger, and any will to action tend to raise the level of the voice. Consider, for example, the pitch which would be natural for Kent's expression of rage toward Cornwall in *King Lear*.

> A plague upon your epileptic visage!
> Smile you my speeches, as I were a fool?
> Goose, if I had you upon Sarum plain,
> I'd drive you cackling home to Camelot.

It would be impossible to give this in a low voice. With the growth of Kent's anger through the scene from which this is excerpted, the level of his tones would tend to rise higher and higher. Consider also the differences of pitch which would certainly be employed by Hamlet between the more and the less active portions of his famous soliloquy spoken after his dismissal of the players in Act II. He accuses himself of cowardice:

> Oh, what a rogue and peasant slave am I!

Now he asks himself how one of the actors would behave if he were in Hamlet's place, driven by the memory of his father's murder.

> What would he do,
> Had he the motive and the cue for passion
> That I have? He would drown the stage with tears
> And cleave the general ear with horrid speech,
> Make mad the guilty and appall the free,
> Confound the ignorant, and amaze indeed
> The very faculties of eyes and ears.

Then, as he contrasts his own behavior, his voice drops.

> Yet I,
> A dull and muddy-mettled rascal, peak,
> Like John-a-dreams, unpregnant of my cause,
> And can say nothing.

Generally speaking, from the point of view of the effect on the listener, high notes tend to be the more exciting. A sports announcer at a football game raises his voice when the ball approaches the goal line. Experiments on dogs have shown that the high, intense tones are associated with alarm, emergency action, whereas low, soft tones produce a feeling of reassurance, calm. It has been noted that the songs of primitive peoples are usually pitched high.[12] There is probably a reason for this; the primitives have learned that on the raised level their songs possess maximum stimulation. In our own operatic forms, the youthful, active, lyrical passages are almost invariably assigned to soprano and tenor voices, whereas the heavier, steadier parts are written for the lower voices.

Although the higher notes tend to be more exciting, they sometimes lack vibrancy, seem less convincing than the medium and lower notes. The deep tones are the body tones. High notes frequently sound as if they sprang from the outside of the speaker's personality, or from his head only, with none of his vital parts participating. An obvious example lies in two renditions of the expression already noted, *I love you.* Given on a very high level, it will usually sound insincere, or at best shallow and sentimental. On a lower level the expression is much more convincing because it suggests that it comes with the whole body behind it.

But one must be very careful to avoid making any stiff generalizations. Variations in pitch produce many different effects. For this reason it would clearly be a mistake for anyone to lay down rules for expressive levels. The setting of pitch and its influence on the listener are conditioned at so many points by character, situation, and secondary factors of impulse and sensation that it is impossible accurately to predict the form in advance of actual speech. The important thing to remember is that variable pitch levels add greatly to the expressive and stimulative influence of speech; and the actor-singer should seek to exploit to the full the dramatic opportunities offered in these changes.

FACTORS IN DESIGN: TIME

Turning to the factor of time, we quickly realize that its influence on dramatic effect is equal to that of pitch. It is as vital a part of song-acting design as it is of dance-acting. As a matter of fact, because the ear is our most sensitive organ for rhythm and tempo, vocal time patterns often set and maintain the form and pace of pantomimic action.

Rhythm, the first phase of the time factor, is essential to effective dialogue. But it must not be regarded as a

FACTORS IN TONAL DESIGN: TIME
Two phases: rhythm and tempo.

special device of dramatic design, for all normal speech —like normal movement—in the everyday world shows a similar pattern of recurring stress. Each of us displays a characteristic rhythm of thought, feeling, and action peculiarly his own. For the portrayal of the stage personality the normal pattern is merely simplified and accentuated a little to increase its effect.

Speech is rhythmic, let us repeat, because thought is rhythmic. When the brain and the body are properly co-ordinated in speech, the rhythmical accent and the thought accent correspond. All good dramatic dialogue, whether in verse or in prose, is written with this recurring accent in mind. An experienced player knows not only how to speak a group of lines with a swing of sound (stressing the emphatic points and subordinating the lesser ones) in such a way that it will be pleasing to listen to, but also how to time his speech so that the key word of each phrase will meet the crest of the wave of the hearer's mental attention—for the audience's attention is also rhythmical. That, of course, is the ultimate reason for the player's use of vocal rhythm.

Dialogue rhythm may or may not be metered. In the performance of Shakespeare and other verse dramas it has, of course, a definite measure.

> JULIET.   Romeo, doff thy name,
> And for that name which is no part of thee
> Take all myself.
> ROMEO.   I take thee at thy word:
> Call me but love, and I'll be new baptized;
> Henceforth I never will be Romeo.

In the rendering of sensitively written prose dialogue, the rhythm is generally freer, less outwardly apparent, but there is the same kind of recurring pause, grouping of sound units, and periodic stress as there is in poetry. The expressive projection of even the most realistic speech requires this kind of rhythmic treatment. Here, for example, is George's description of ranch hands in John Steinbeck's play *Of Mice and Men:*

> Guys like us that work on ranches is the loneliest guys in the world. They ain't got no family. They don't belong no place. They come to a ranch and work up a stake and then

they go in to town and blow up a stake. And then the first thing you know they're pounding their tail on some other ranch. They ain't got nothin' to look ahead to.[13]

And here are a few lines, with stage directions and quotation marks omitted, from the end of the same play:

LENNIE. Tell how it's gonna be.

GEORGE. Look acrost the river, Lennie, and I'll tell you like you can almost see it. We gonna get a little place. . . .

LENNIE. Go on! Go on! How's it gonna be? We gonna get a little place. . . .

GEORGE. We'll have a cow. And we'll have maybe a pig and chickens—and down the flat we'll have a . . . little piece of alfalfa. . . .

LENNIE. For the rabbits!

GEORGE. For the rabbits!

LENNIE. And I get to tend the rabbits?

GEORGE. And you get to tend the rabbits!

LENNIE. And live on the fat o' the land!

GEORGE. Yes. Look over there, Lennie. Like you can really see it.

LENNIE. Where?

GEORGE. Right acrost the river there. Can't you almost see it?

LENNIE. Where, George?

GEORGE. It's over there. You keep lookin', Lennie. Just keep lookin'.

LENNIE. I'm lookin', George, I'm lookin'.

GEORGE. That's right. It's gonna be nice there. Ain't gonna be no trouble, no fights. Nobody ever gonna hurt nobody, or steal from 'em. It's gonna be—nice.

LENNIE. I can see it, George. I can see it! Right over there! I can see it![14]

The vocal rhythms in effective dialogue may at times be hardly perceptible as design; yet, as one listens, one will sense below the words two or more pulsating drives, one for the lines of each character. The rhythms move the speeches along. The different fundamental "swings" are harmonized to make the larger rhythmic pattern of this scene. In other scenes the pattern will doubtless change, though certain features of the master rhythm will continue throughout the play to give the whole its own peculiar individuality. The absence of rhythmic patterns is one of the surest give-aways of both inexperienced playwriting and inexperienced acting.

Tempo, or rate, which regulates speed, must be distinguished from rhythm, the pattern of time. Tempo is checked against the passing accents. The correct tempo for a speech, or a set of speeches, is commonly determined from the rate of breathing felt to be appropriate to the situation being played.

In *Beauty and Human Nature*, Albert Chandler has drawn attention to the psychological effects of different tempos in music. Rapid notes, he shows, tend to contribute to the expression of gaiety, agitation, threatened approach, terrified flight, or any other kind of general tension. A slower tempo, on the other hand, adds to the expression of majestic motion, reverie, despair, any relaxation of tension.[15] This observation richly suggests the effects of changing tempo in speech. The quicker rhythms, like the higher pitches, commonly express tension, whereas the slower patterns, like the lower levels of tone, tell of relaxed tension. The whole effects of the examples we

have used to illustrate pitch changes certainly depend
also on tempo changes as contributing factors.

Tempo is an extremely important element of stage
speech. In fact, the sense of tempo is regarded by many as
a first index of dramatic instinct. Certainly no actor who
lacks it has ever achieved success.

FACTORS IN DESIGN: FORCE

The factors of pitch and time are closely associated with
a third, force. The three operate together, modifying and
reinforcing each other's stimulative and expressive contri-
butions. Broadly speaking, changes of pitch and time, as
we have seen, tend to indicate variations of general tension in the attitude of the speaker. Changes of force are
commonly expressive of the same alterations.

But increased force is not necessarily connected with
rising notes and rapid tempo—though the union is common, as when one "raises one's voice." Force is often
associated with a low voice speaking in slow tempo. This
is especially true when the tone is considered characteristic
of a certain personality. More general strength, earthy
vitality, is usually attributed to the man with the slow bass
voice, and the woman with the contralto, than to the
man and woman with the tenor and soprano.

Like force in dance acting, force in song acting has two
aspects. They are gross volume and intensity. The experienced player differentiates carefully between them.
When a character on the stage employs volume, he may
command a great crowd, call a long distance, or hurl loud

defiance at an opponent. When, on the other hand, the
force of his action is marked by intensity, he may use a
very little voice. A whisper may carry such intensity that
the listener will be stirred to the depths of his nature.

Much emphasis has been laid by experienced speakers
on the need for relaxation. But the difference between
vocal relaxation and vocal collapse is carefully noted. In
vibrant speech there is always a sense of aliveness. Whether
the actor utters his words loudly or in the faintest whisper,

FACTORS IN TONAL DESIGN: FORCE
Two phases: volume and intensity.

there is a feeling of strength. Even when the actor is playing the role of a very lazy tramp yawning in the sun, and
everything seen and heard upon the stage denotes relaxation, there must be, underlying and supporting the sleepy
voice coming over the footlights, some residue of vibrant
tension. If there is none, the scene may become "realis-
tically representative," but dramatically it will be dead.
When a capable pianist plays the drowsy passages of a
lullaby, he does not for an instant relax the pressure of his
fingers on the keys. He simply creates the *impression* of
sleepiness. There lies the difference between reality and
art. The singer-actor must seize and hold the whole
space around him in exactly the same way as the dancer-

actor. He must fill it with his tone, even when he whispers, so that the personality of the character he portrays, his desires, his pain, his joy may transcend the little body on the stage and touch the fringes of the cosmic.

A common fault of both the professional and the amateur speaker is to withdraw support from their expressive tones before they have finished a thought. A star actor in a recent leading Broadway play showed this weakness conspicuously. In a single passage he spoke the ends of forty-two consecutive sentences down, without one upward inflection. It could be argued that, because the scene showed a character in a discouraged mood, the actor turned his sentences down deliberately. If the forty-two consecutive drops were intentional, I feel that this actor failed to distinguish clearly in his mind between a superficial trick of characterization and fundamental auditory design. The very fact that the downward inflections were so noticeable that they had to be counted shows that he failed. True characterization never demands a weakness in tonal music.

THE TWO PRIMARY
INFLUENCES ON SONG ACTING

The observation was made in the preceding chapter that there are two primary influences working on human behavior: biology, and society. The first is connected with the natural, primitive side of man, his urges for bodily welfare in relationship to his physical environment. The

actions which reflect the biological drive are gross, free,
often violent. The second, or social, influence is associated
with man's adjustment to other men, and is manifested
in the modifications, particularly the restraints, imposed
upon the primitive actions.

Biology and society, which shape the forms of dance
acting, control also the tonal designs of song acting. Vocal
sounds spring naturally from the same impulses that move
the body. So, when the trunk, the head, the arms and legs
are stirred into big action by the inward movement of
biological drives, the voice also tends to be free. The inflectional ranges are wide; the changes between the different pitch, time, and force elements are vigorous, explicit.
Tone qualities are indicative of keen sensuous activity.
The whole organization of sound speaks frankly of desires,
and of a directness of effort to gratify those desires. But
when the influence of society places a check upon physical
action, it modifies also the vocal patterns. The sensuous
tones are less frank, and the vocal reflection of dynamic
urges is discreetly controlled. In cases of extreme restraint
—when, for example, a private in the army answers an
officer, or a witness replies in court—the vocal design may
be flattened out almost completely.

Fine song acting, like fine dance acting, maintains an
eloquent balance between the forces of biology and society. In the vocal portrayal of simple, natural characters,
the basic urges to resist gravity, to move toward appealing
objects, to retreat from repugnant presences, to touch desirable things, and to wrestle with or destroy inimical ones,
will be more evident. In the portrayal of a sophisticated
citizen of the world, the freer vocal movements reflecting

the primitive urges will, perhaps, be absent. But the tone play of dramatic speech can never be neutral. Even when a highly "cultivated" gentleman or lady is shown trying to hide feelings beneath a flat vocal lid, there should be some telltale hints—through slight overemphasis, or intensity, say—which will reveal, by implication, the larger pattern, the larger feeling, not directly indicated. As we have said before, the *image* of the savage beneath the skin of the gentleman or lady should always be clear.

THE SINGER-ACTOR'S TRAINING

The training of the singer-actor closely parallels that of the dancer-actor, particularly where it touches the development of sensory awareness. All the exercises the player gives himself to sharpen up his pantomimic responses to stimuli of sight, touch, taste, and smell, as well as sound, will greatly extend his tonal vocabulary. If he can make himself *feel* clearly the reaction of his body to the bigness, highness, nearness, sharpness, heat, odor, as well as the sound, of the presences he meets and the presences he remembers, his words are bound to have color. Sensuous vibrancy in the actor's body compels vivid speech.

But after the player has developed a live body and learned to feel his voice united with it, he cannot expect to command his whole latent range of expressiveness until he trains his instrument. As a speaker, he must study the articulative form of words, so that he can project them clearly, easily; and then, as a singer, he must learn how to surround them with tone, play melodies with them, and develop from them a song. He must educate his vocal apparatus to give at command any note out of an octave and a half or two octaves, and to move his words over a wide range of time and force.

The vocal members involved in the training include the jaws, the lips, the tongue, the muscles of the throat, the muscles of the chest, the diaphragm, and the upper abdomen. More than that, they include all the muscles of the body connected with posture and movement. And, most of all, they include the ear, for until the ear has been educated to hear critically the sounds of the speaker's voice, all his other efforts are fruitless.

The price of easy and flexible control is, of course, long, hard work. The guidance of a competent speech teacher is indispensable. But the program of training does not end with this phase of study. The ambitious player supplements the basic exercises in voice and diction with at least some singing. And on every possible occasion he listens to music of all kinds, trying to discover the secret of its effects in order to make them his own.

SONG ACTING AND
DANCE ACTING UNITED

The techniques of dance acting and song acting have been analyzed separately, but they are, of course, parts of the same expressive method. For this reason they should al-

ways, in practice, be considered together. There is little
danger of the two phases of acting becoming dissociated
if the player and the director remember to do two things:
(1) design the pantomime to evoke auditive images, flood
the stage with silent song; (2) speak to the eye of the
spectator, make him see actions beyond those given by
the body of the performer. In this way dance acting and
song acting will fulfill mutually their common functions
of stimulation and expression.

Chapter Five

ACTION

THE DESIRE FOR ACTION

In the opening pages of this book members of an imaginary audience were asked the question, "What draws you to the theatre?" They replied in effect, "The satisfaction of three desires: diversion, stimulation, and clarification." And they explained that these three words stood generally for interesting characters, a good story, some comments about human nature and the world around us; and also the way, or manner, in which these were presented on the stage.

If the questioning had been pushed a little farther, it would have revealed that the three fundamental desires just mentioned spring from another desire still more basic, the desire for a *quickening of the sense of living*. The passionate craving to feel active is a part of human nature. Man is a restless creature, full of driving urges. Every hour of his waking life he seeks to move, to use his abilities, to express in a hundred ways the many aspects of his personality. When his impulses to be doing are frustrated, and, because of the behavior of others or the failure of his own powers, he is unable to fulfill desire by overt action, he tends to turn for compensatory satisfaction—and often for help—to the imaginative world of the theatre. There, as in no other place, a common man may feel the stir of all his faculties. By imagination he holds communion with the creative mind of the author. He plays along with the characters in their adventures, participating or commenting. He unites himself with the swinging words and pantomime of the actors, and feels as if he himself had deftly directed the action, composed the music, painted the settings. He is lifted, because he is animated. Every part of him—playboy, dreamer, philosopher, and artist—is exercised. He sees clearly, he speaks persuasively, he strides across the world like a man of consequence doing the many shrewd, daring, important things he has never quite been able to perform outside the theatre. Even if the individual is one of those rarely fortunate persons who are able to discharge in action most of their primary desires, he still finds a sense of *quickening* in the theatre—the best of it—for there is no man breathing whose strength for life is equal to his appetite.

The first problem of dramatic craftsmanship, then, is to discover the secret of *action*; until that is found, any effort to build up a stage technique is bound to be meaningless.

THE THREE
KINDS OF ACTION

That action is the basic substance of drama is, of course, no new conclusion. This was realized thousands of years ago. The very word *drama* is dynamic, meaning "some-

Thomas Bouchard

ACTION

Movement in space in a conquest of gravity: the Humphrey-Weidman Group in *New Dance*.

ACTION

Transit in space, in a pursuit of adjustment. The player is moving over the ground, and, at the same time, he is trying to achieve something anticipated by the spectator. *Ball Carrier*, a lithograph by Benton Spruance.

thing done"—in contrast with something merely talked
about. But few of those who have captured the *idea* of action and bound it to a sheet of paper have been able to give
a comprehensive view of it. The reason doubtless is that
most writers on the subject have attempted to see it as
one thing, when in reality it is several things—or, more
accurately, perhaps, one thing with several phases.

What are the phases of action in the theatre? Analysis
shows, I think, that there are at least three: transit, change,
and pursuit of adjustment; and that every dramatic scene
is founded on at least one, commonly on all three of them.

ACTION CONCEIVED AS TRANSIT

Transit, the first phase of action, is simple motion. An
object shifts its position in relationship to the objects
around it. It "goes." The movement may be extended or
limited, rapid or slow, along a straight or an irregular
path, it matters little; while there is transit there is activity.
Because man is a restless individual, this phase is close to
his impulses, and the sense of it is dear to him. It is impossible for him to stand still for any length of time, since
his feet and legs are constructed for moving. He cannot
even sit still. In a set of experiments it was found that the
average person could remain physically motionless for
only a brief period.* Even such individuals as artists'

* Subjects, seated in a chair, were instructed to refrain from changing
their positions. They could not. The average interval of immobility
was only 1.8 minutes, the range being from 3.6 seconds to 5 minutes.

models, who are especially trained to hold one pose for fifteen minutes or half an hour at a time, have to engage their bodies in at least a little movement, sometimes shifting their weight slightly from one foot to the other, sometimes flexing or unflexing their fingers. But these limited changes of position never bring great satisfaction. One

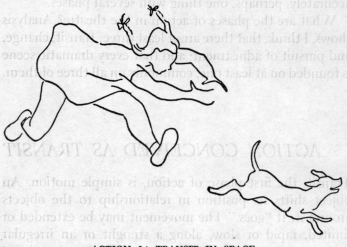

ACTION 1: TRANSIT IN SPACE

feels fully, gloriously alive only when the body is moving freely—striding along a country road, climbing a rocky hill, or playing a fast game of tennis. It is an exciting experience to run, to cover ground, to consume and conquer space with the power of one's own muscles. It is almost as exciting to be borne through space on a swift vehicle— especially when one's body controls that vehicle. Hence comes man's extraordinary love for racing boats, motorcars, airplanes.

ACTION 1: TRANSIT IN SPACE

The personal experiences to which this gives rise breed
a ready appreciation of transit in other bodies. Long ago,
psychology recognized the fact that movement is a deter-
mining factor in attracting attention. A moving object
is far more likely to be noticed than a still one. Ship-
wrecked men wave their shirts to attract the sight of passing ships. A deer in the woods remains unnoticed by the

ACTION 1: TRANSIT IN SPACE

Dancers in a Negro revue, sketched by Betty Joiner. (Reproduced by
courtesy of *Theatre Arts Monthly*.)

huntsman until it starts to run. Anyone who has observed
a dog stalking a squirrel in a park knows clearly the relative
influences of motion and stillness. The dog approaches
swiftly when the squirrel's eyes are turned away, but the
instant the squirrel faces about the dog "freezes" his whole
body, often leaving a paw half in air. By instinct he knows
that movement will make the squirrel notice him.

Man's desire for the sense of transit in the field of entertainment is demonstrated in his fondness for ferris wheels, merry-go-rounds, loop-the-loops, boat rides, car rides, and the sight of race horses and fast games. It explains to a great extent the attraction of boxing bouts, the circus, and vaudeville. In the theatre it explains the popularity of "screw-ball" comedies, slapstick films, and many of the melodramas.

While the design of the more "serious" dramatic performances does not always accept the immediate value of the rough-and-tumble type of transit action, it does admit the necessity of some kind of outward movement. Nothing is more deadening to the senses than a long scene in which two people stand or sit in one position. An adroit director contrives to employ at least a modicum of physical movement in every scene, even in the comparatively static expository passages, not only because a mobile body in a speaker helps to make what he has to say stimulatingly expressive, but also because motion of any kind helps to keep the senses of the spectators alert. A skillful actor can usually suggest more of transit action than is actually stated; but he must make *some* of it manifest to supply a clue for the rest.

ACTION CONCEIVED AS CHANGE

That motion in three-dimensional space (or transit, as we are calling it here) does not account for the whole secret of dramatic action is obvious. The chorus numbers in a musical revue are always exciting, for a while. If they continued to hold the stage indefinitely they would be boring, and everyone would be tempted to cry out, "Let's get on with the show!" Many plays, unintelligently filled with much "stage business"—ceaseless risings, sittings, crossings—fail entirely in their intentions, seem monotonous. They never "get anywhere." There is, therefore, the second phase of dramatic action to be recognized—that is, action conceived as *change*. The quality of something alters, or one object is substituted for another; and in the

ACTION 2: CHANGE

An object the quality of which alters in a marked way—even if the object does not move in space—is active. Example: a blinking light bulb. (To sense the action in the drawing, the reader should look at the lamps, not all together, but in sequence.)

presence of that shift, the senses and the mind of the person impressed are excited. There is a feeling of activity.

The difference between action conceived as *transit* and action conceived as *change* may be illustrated in two electric signs. They both have a border of blinking bulbs; but in one the design runs round and round, while in the other it stands in one position and comes and goes. Both of the signs are active, but in different ways; one by way of movement through space, the other by way of alternating impressions.

Of course, the two phases of action are not antithetical; they may be combined in a single object. A distance runner on a cinder path, for instance, is observed to be jogging along for some time at a certain speed, then suddenly, as he approaches the finish, to shift his gait and spurt toward the tape. The change of speed is arresting, and produces in the spectator a sense of activity beyond that given

ACTION 2: CHANGE

A number of dead clock faces placed next to one another may seem to be active simply because of the variations in the positions of the hands. (To sense action in this drawing, the reader should not look at all the faces as a group, but should move his eyes quickly from one to another in any direction.)

simply by the runner's passage along the track. The effect here comes from the *increase* in motion. A similar or equivalent effect may be obtained by just the opposite means, the *stoppage* of motion. A man, walking back and forth across the room, suddenly stands still. Here again there is action, because of a marked alteration in the quality of the stimuli provided by the walker. The observer takes notice that something has happened. Both of these instances, the one of the man's increasing motion, and the one of the man's ceasing motion, are founded on transit action; but they derive their special effect from change of impression.

A strong sense of action may spring from objects far less stimulating for their own sakes than blinking light bulbs or runners on tracks. The sudden appearance of a cat in a chair, the quick vision of a bird on the window sill, the swift vanishing of sunlight behind a cloud, these may be exciting. Even simple shapes in a pictural design, say an advertisement, may have action. As the eye of the observer progresses around the design, it finds a black area, then a white area, then an orange shape contrasted with a blue, a straight line butted smartly against a curved line, and so on. The "reading" of the advertisement becomes therefore a sort of adventure, through the *activity of change.*

So far, reference has been made to visual impressions only. It is scarcely necessary to point out that there may be a sense of change activity in taste, touch, and hearing equivalent to that for sight. This is particularly true in hearing. Consider the stir in the listener caused by the sound of a voice in the stillness of night, the sudden call of a bugle. Musical design depends for some of its most striking effects on the "action" sensed when one key shifts into another, and when dissonances are resolved into consonances. The whole tonal structure built out of changes of pitch and quality is basically active.

Exactly the same kind of observation can be made, of course, about all the visual and auditory details in a stage

performance. When the play and its acting are well designed, the audience senses with excitement the many big
and little changes of inflection, pitch, and time between
speech and speech; the contrasting patterns of gesture
between character and character, and in each character
individually; and the varying volume, intensity, and emotional quality of the different scenes as a whole. When all
these elements are skillfully handled to make each set off
the next (in the right proportion) through the effect of
change, a tremendous sense of activity is created.

It is especially the appropriate, but *unexpected*, details
which produce the keenest effect. A character, seated for
some time, leaps to his feet. A man interrupts a quiet
gathering by rushing in through the door. A person speaking on one level suddenly drops his voice to another. But
the effect of action is not necessarily dependent on violent
changes. The appearance of anything new, different from
that which has gone before (provided the new element is
presented with the right degree of smartness), gives the
observer the same kind of feeling. In this respect, the
recent production of Thornton Wilder's "quiet" play,
Our Town, in New York was full of action. There were
many appropriate, but unexpected, details. Anyone who
saw the play will remember them: the crisp entrance of
the milkman with the invisible but audible milk bottles;
the sudden clucking of the imaginary chickens; the professor's statistical information (quite fitting but unantici-
pated); the momentary glimpse of the choir in the pit; the
Stage Manager's stepping in to play the part of the drug
clerk, and his later appearance as the preacher; Mrs. Gibb's
calling George back, on his wedding morning, to put on

ACTION 2: CHANGE

Although each of the poses, viewed simply, is static, it seems, in combination with the others, to be active because of its difference. Many of the sequence drawings in cartoon strips use dramatically the principle of change illustrated here.

his rubbers; many of the quietly unexpected remarks of the Stage Manager. These were just a few of the larger devices which kept alive sensuously the anticipatory interest of the audience. There were, of course, a hundred other details less surprising perhaps than these, but all strongly effective in creating a sense of action through change. Sometimes this sense was produced by an alteration in outward presences (as in most of the illustrations noted), sometimes simply by a shift in direction of a thought (as in the Stage Manager's remarks). In either case, the essential activity lay not in the external factors of speech and gesture, but in the marked turn of the observer's state of mind. At every point where his attitude was made to shift, there was activity.

Variety is not only the spice of life; it is also a necessity. It has already been suggested that the business of the theatre is to find and satisfy the fundamental cravings of people for a feeling of liveness. Because change is a primary factor in keeping our senses keen, our minds alert, it is basic to all dramatic effect.

ACTION CONCEIVED
AS PURSUIT OF ADJUSTMENT

The activity of transit through space and the activity of change do not provide the whole activity appeal of the theatre. If they did, people would be content to see nothing but circuses and revues; for these two forms have both

kinds of action in abundance. Stimulating as circuses and
revues are, however, they all have one serious lack. They
"get nowhere." Consequently, the dramatic artists must
recognize a third important aspect of action. It is the one
which gives extended performances a sense of direction, a
sense of meaning. For want of a better term, we will call
it action conceived as *pursuit of adjustment.*

In *Art as Experience,* John Dewey points out that man,
like the lower animals, lives not merely *in* an environment,
but because of it, through interaction with it. "Life grows,"
he says, "when a temporary falling out is a transition to a
more extensive balance of the energies of the organism
with those of the conditions under which it lives." [1]
Dewey's description of the effort of the human organism
to adjust itself to its environment gives us our best clue
to the real essence of movement. That essence lies in *pursuit of adjustment.* When the human organism is, comparatively speaking, in equilibrium with its environment,
it seeks no action for itself, neither transit nor change; it
does not even desire the quickening sense of action in
other bodies. It is quite content to sit quietly, without
exerting itself in any way. But such a condition rarely
occurs. Most of the time, man is seeking one, and another,
and then another adjustment to his surroundings. Out of
that constant pursuit come his own struggling efforts, and
likewise his interest in every other organism which is seeking an adjustment. Putting it simply, we can say that every
kind of object which appears to an observer to be out of
equilibrium with its environment, and to be on the point
of trying to re-establish that equilibrium, has in it the

potentialities for movement. Movement is seen when the adjustment is in progress. The object may be a person. It may be an animal. It may be a piece of furniture; it may be a graphic design. It may even be just a line in that design.

The accompanying drawings illustrate how the principles of adjustment and motion apply in three different

ACTION 3: PURSUIT, OR ANTICIPATION, OF ADJUSTMENT

The figure above is implicitly active, because it is in a position it cannot maintain. The man must make an adjustment in one of two ways: (1) by falling to the floor, or (2) by throwing one leg back to support his weight.

objects. In the first, the figure of the man is depicted in a seated attitude, but without a chair. Both physically and emotionally this posture is manifestly out of balance with the present environment. An adjustment is bound to take place in one of two ways: the man will fall, or, what is

more likely if his faculties are alive, he will thrust a leg
back to hold himself. In either case there is motion—in
one without, and in one with, the will of the man.

In the second drawing the object out of equilibrium
with respect to its surroundings is inanimate, simply a
weight on one side of a pair of scales. The arm holding

ACTION 3: PURSUIT, OR ANTICIPATION, OF ADJUSTMENT

The scale arm is implicitly active, because the weighted side, without
support, cannot maintain its present position.

the weight is up. Obviously it cannot remain in this position. An adjustment is bound to take place, and that
adjustment will require motion.

But the object felt to be on the point of movement need
not, as we have suggested, be anything so concrete as a
man or a weight on a pair of scales. It can be just a line.
This is illustrated in the third drawing. The vertical and
the horizontal lines seem "adjusted"; so they are "quiet."
But the line drawn on an angle appears to be exposed to
the force of gravity. "It cannot remain in that position,"
we seem to say to ourselves. "It is searching for rest," or,
"It is rising from rest." So it is "active." The four drawings on page 152 show how different with respect to the
sense of movement two treatments of the same basic de-

sign may be. In two of the drawings the lines are established, "adjusted"; in the others they appear to be on the point of going somewhere—up or down or around to another position, searching for rest. One feels that, if one closed one's eyes for a moment and then opened them,

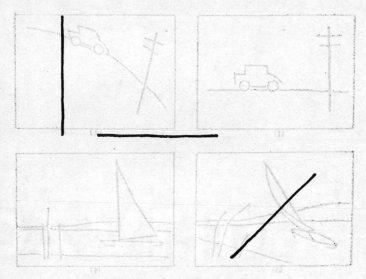

STILL AND ACTIVE LINES

The perpendicular line in a graphic design commonly seems to be established, while the horizontal line is at rest, and the diagonal line is active (because it looks as if it were rising or falling).

he would find that the pictures had changed. This principle of activity in lines is used constantly in advertising —because real or implied movement is always more arresting than stillness. Other forces, of course, than that of gravity are often employed. Conspicuous voids, or centers of attraction, may be established, and certain elements of the drawing may appear to be trying to move toward them; or colors in a series may seem to be "reaching" for a tonal equilibrium; and so on.

In the several illustrations just given, the *pursuit of adjustment* has been external.* But a sense of activity is

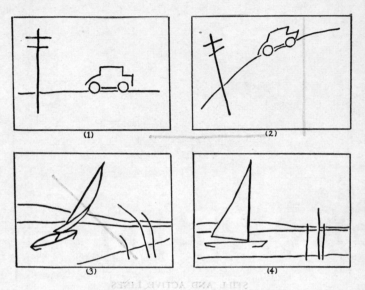

THE DIAGONAL LINE IS ACTIVE

Comparison in graphic design between compositions constructed on straight and those constructed on slanting lines. The shapes in 2 and 3 look more active than those in 1 and 4 simply because the former seem not yet to have reached a state of rest. They are in process of adjustment.

not dependent solely on a manifestation of gravity, or on any other purely outward tug. The operating force may be

* Also they have all been visual. But in the world of sound we find equivalent pursuits of adjustment; example, the unresolved chord in music.

psychological. A homely example can be found in the kitchen. The soup starts to burn. Viewed from a purely physical point of view, there is nothing conspicuously out of equilibrium in the situation. If the soup remains on the fire, no object will fall, the cook will remain standing where she is, by the sink. Psychologically, however, the

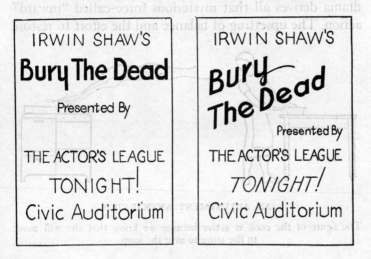

THE DIAGONAL LINE IS ACTIVE
A comparison between the effects made by horizontal and diagonal lettering in a poster.

situation is radically out of balance. The cook cannot remain still with the knowledge that supper is being ruined on the stove. In a desperate attempt to restore equilibrium, she rushes over to rescue the soup. Any portion of the scene is active up to the moment when the soup is removed from the fire and the cook recognizes that it is safe. If the soup is indeed safe, activity (from the psychological viewpoint) is over. If, however, the flavor of the soup is found to be impaired, and the cook feels the necessity for preparing another pot of it, the cook's sense of adjustment with respect to one point in her environment is again destroyed, and again there is activity.

It is from the pursuit of psychological adjustment that drama derives all that mysterious force called "inward" action. The upsetting of balance and the effort to restore

AN ADJUSTMENT ANTICIPATED

The figure of the cook is active because we know that she will move to the stove to save the soup.

it commonly involve issues more complex than that of the burning soup; but the principle underlying the sense of dramatic activity is the same. A recognition of this will help to answer that question which has perplexed so many authors and actors: why are some pauses on the stage felt to be "moving," while others are just pauses? A pause is pregnant with action when it continues a sense of emotional unbalance previously established, and, by the stillness, it suggests that an agony of perplexity has momentarily inhibited all outward sound or motion. Breathlessly,

the spectator waits to see what visible and audible shapes
the pursuit of readjustment will take.

It is for this reason that the half-inarticulate passages
of many plays are dramatically the most stirring. The pain
of ill adjustment and the longing for some hoped-for solution lie too deep for facile expression. The performance of
Our Town, to which reference has already been made, was
full of such scenes: the end of the first act when the boy,
George Gibbs, and the girl, Emily Webb, knelt by their
windows in the spring moonlight, and tried to find the
answer to their youthful longings; the scene at the drug
counter, where brokenly they attempted to express their
desires for each other; but especially that moment in the
church when the two young people, cut adrift from the
security of family ties, faced each other across the aisle,
their young stomachs sucked up in the pain of frightened
loneliness, and looked to each other for help. The sense of
action marched on irresistibly until the preacher pronounced them married, and the two hastened brightly
down the aisle and away. And still there was something
left to be completed. Because the audience felt that there
were yet environmental forces with which George and
Emily must reckon before they could find rest, it eagerly
awaited the last act.

All action involves at least an implicit recognition of
time. Therefore, action is most powerfully manifested in
the so-called "time arts": music, dance, drama. In them
the observer has an opportunity to watch and hear, with
anticipatory excitement, not one act of adjustment, but
an unfolding series. This is especially true in the theatre.
Conceived in its most elemental terms, a play depicts,

through sight and sound, the progressive adventures of a human organism driven by a desire to make some kind of important adjustment. The dramatic artist who keeps this in mind will never have to inquire the way to action.

Chapter Six

COMPOSITION

THE PLAYWRIGHT,
THE ACTOR, AND THE DIRECTOR

Someone has defined the successful performance of a play as an "effect made upon an audience." [1] It is a good description. Viewed in the light, not of those who act, but of those who respond, an "effective" performance is a single, synthesized impression built up from movement and sound, color and light, put together in accordance with a certain plan. *Design* dictates this plan. The chief dramatic composers involved are three: the playwright, the actor, and the director.*

The playwright is the visionary, the actor is the executor. The director is the intermediary and co-ordinator between the two. Often he is more than that, an original artist in his own right. Thinking in large images beyond the first creation of the playwright, he often inspires and leads the author into new stretches of composition. Examples of this type of collaboration are seen daily in Hollywood and New York. Not infrequently the director is also, in a practical sense, the basic actor, setting the form

---

* Because they do not fit exactly into this present discussion, we are omitting here the three important technical artists, the designers of scenery, lighting, and costumes.

and tone for every part of the dramatic translation. More
often he stands as a sort of middleman, or arbiter, between
the author and the player. His function is to take the sheaf
of lettered symbols prepared by the playwright, re-envision
from them the living pictures conceived therein, and then
decide how most effectively the creative resources of a
body of actors may be exploited to bring the vision into
actual being. In a sense he is the conductor of a dramatic
orchestra. Like his colleague in the musical field, he may
not dictate a single note, or offer a single suggestion regarding specific techniques, and yet remain the central
figure in the rendition. The director brings out, subdues,
accents, develops, brings all together, keeps all the parts
in proportion, guides every player in the upward progress
toward the climactic moments.

If the director is arbiter and guide for the artists,
he is first of all the chief representative of the spectators. As he sits in a seat "out front" directing the action on the stage, he conceives himself to be the most
sensitive and critical member of the prospective audience, and he checks against the responses of that spectator every part of the unfolding design. In the light of
those reactions, he points up the action here, subordi-
nates it there, reshapes this movement here, reorders that
sequence of sounds there, gives thought to balance, proportion, and growth, continuing his experiments until he
feels himself dancing and singing with the actors in the
way he hopes, and, if he is an experienced director, he
knows the audience will dance and sing. Thus he col-
laborates with the author and the actor in the production
of the "effect."

The preceding chapters have dealt with the individual actor's technique. The remainder of this book is written especially for the director. It is intended to provide, not a body of rules, but some provocative suggestions for the translation of a playwright's "score" into a well-orchestrated performance. The players in that performance are dancers and singers.

PRINCIPLES OF ORDER: CONTRAST

Dramatic design for the director comprises two processes, selection and arrangement.

Having picked the elements with which he intends to work, the designer-director faces the problem of composing them. He must proportion each part, place it so that it will most forcefully set off other parts and point toward the climaxes. To help him in his composition, he has at his disposal several universal "principles of order."

The two most important principles are *contrast* and *unity*. We will limit our consideration first to contrast. Contrast is the life of art. Monotony is destructive to attention. The processes of the human organism involved in attending are never in a stationary balance. Consequently, the mind of man cannot remain fastened to any one little phase of an object observed for more than a few seconds at a time. It has to move. We cannot look long at the nose on a man's face without looking at his mouth and eyes.

We cannot view his face for any length of time without glancing at his body. Continued attention needs plenty of stimuli, each operating newly and freshly. Anything which fails to provide these *different* appeals to our senses of sight or hearing tends, therefore, to lose our interest.

We cannot concentrate long on the photograph of a man. Why? Because the figure never changes the posture of its body. And it never says anything. If we were told that we must look at that picture for fifteen minutes without lifting our eyes from it to any other object in the room, we should soon find ourselves growing very weary. In spite of the fact that we had our eyes fastened on the picture, our minds would wander elsewhere before very long, and if we determined not to let attention shift, but to keep it nailed to the object at which we were looking, we should probably go to sleep.

Objects do not have to be still to bore us. Who can gaze for long at a swinging pendulum or at a man who is simply moving his arm up and down? Equally dulling to the senses are the stimuli offered by unchanging sounds —the whir of a motor, the patter of rain, the droning voice of a preacher or lecturer. The effects produced by sameness of sensory appeal operate just as strongly in figures of art as in the objects of natural life. A drawing with all the lines running in a single direction, or a painting rendered without changes of value, is not very interesting; neither is a piece of music which is all in one time, and which repeats one section over and over again.

Without change, diversity of effects, there can be no sustained attention. There we see one of the fundamental reasons for the necessity of contrast. But that is not the only one. There is another one, even more fundamental. *Contrast* is the central aspect of form. Where there is no contrast there can be really no shape at all, because there is no basis for comparison. Daylight would have no significance without the alternate contrast of night; years would cease to be years if there were no summers and winters. There could be no continents without land and water; no mountains without the contrasting valleys. There could be no life without youth and age; no wisdom without knowledge and ignorance; no morality without right and wrong. Contrast, a manifested differentiation between the qualities of things, must, therefore, be the first law of form. Between opposites there may be, of course, an infinite number of gradations, "shadings." But none of these has meaning without the contrasts from which it is derived, and with which it is compared.

The operation of the principle of opposing values which may be observed in the forces of the external world, and in the aspects of man's objective thought regarding these forces, is also to be found lying deep within man's body and soul. In fact, it is his sense of inner contrasts which probably gives man his poignant understanding of external differences. Through every moment of his conscious existence he feels in his flesh and spirit the presence of conflicting influences, all of which are related in one way or another to heightened or lowered animation. His basic impulses are appetencies and aversions, born of his sense of these "good" and "bad" influences. From the action of the alternating impulses are derived man's changing moods, his opposing passions.

All designs begin, then, with contrast—for two reasons.

Contrast attracts attention, and it makes form clear. Let
us observe how the artist employs this principle in different fields of expressive effort. The elements composed by
the painter are line, mass, space, and color. These he
compares one with another—line with line, mass with
mass, space with space, color with color—in a scheme of
design ordered by contrast. And the artist compares not
only line with line, mass with mass, and space with space,
but also line with mass, mass with space, and so on, in such
a way as to open up in the picture limitless variations in
form. The drawings opposite show how the principle of
contrast is employed in the composition of a picture.

In his arrangement of the contour lines and mass parts
of a figure in stone or bronze, the sculptor uses the same
principle of contrast. Architectural objects offer probably
the clearest examples of form constructed from opposing
elements. Note how even in the simplest building the
horizontal lines of the foundation and eaves, and those
marking the edges of the sills and lintels of the doors and
windows, are set off against the vertical lines represented
by the corners of the house and the sides of the openings.
In contrast, again, to the right-angle lines of the block of
the house, there are the oblique lines of the roof. As the
design of the building is elaborated, the application of
the principle of contrast is extended. The rectilinear shape
of the main entrance, perhaps, is differentiated from that
of the other doors and of the windows by the addition
of a pediment; curved motifs are employed to relieve the
monotony of the straight; supplementary porches, columns, arches, and specially decorated cornices are used to
offset plain walls; and so on.

Contrast in poetry and music is almost too obvious to require pointing out. There could be no meter, or beaten measures of any kind, without accents; and accents imply, of course, a differentiation between "strong" and "weak." The higher variations in music occur in the "statement"

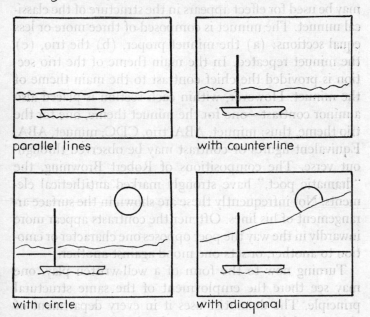

parallel lines   with counterline

with circle   with diagonal

THE DEVELOPMENT OF A PICTORIAL DESIGN THROUGH PROGRESSIVE CONTRASTS

The first arrangement is based on parallel horizontal lines. The second plan exploits a perpendicular line running counter to the horizontal. The third contrasts the straight lines with a circle. The fourth plan shows another contrast in the diagonal. Carried still a step further, this simple pictorial design would be enriched by a contrast between masses of dark and light, and then by contrasts in pigmentary color. The same principle of progressive planning can be used in the development of stage scenery or stage action.

and "contrast" sections of song forms, the first and second themes of sonatas, the verses and choruses of ballads, the "slow" and "fast" movements of symphonies. Such examples are inexhaustible. One of the most perfect illustrations of how both major and minor opposing elements may be used for effect appears in the structure of the classical minuet. The minuet is composed of three more or less equal sections: (a) the minuet proper, (b) the trio, (c) the minuet repeated. In the main theme of the trio section is provided the chief contrast to the main theme of the minuet. However, within each section is placed also a minor contrast—one for the minuet theme, one for the trio theme, thus: minuet, ABA; trio, CDC; minuet, ABA. Equivalent figures of contrast may be observed throughout verse. The compositions of Robert Browning, the "dramatic poet," have strongly marked antithetical elements. Not infrequently these are shown in the surface arrangement of his lines. Oftener the contrasts appear more inwardly in the way the poet opposes one character or emotion to another, or sets one mood against another.

Turning now to the form of a well-written play, one may see there the employment of the same structural principle. The dramatist uses it in every department of character delineation and plot development. Contrast is the tissue of drama. The examples of its value which might be cited are limited only by the number of differentiated personalities, events, actions, and speeches recorded in all theatre literature. Turn to the bookshelf and pick up the first volume of plays. Shakespeare is the most available. Take *Macbeth*. The whole nature of the dramatic story in this play is suggested in the contradictory words uttered by the witches almost as the curtain rises: "Fair is foul, and foul is fair." Macbeth has "reaped golden opinions of all sorts of people" when the story opens, but, before the final scene has been played, his name has become the vilest of reproaches among men. Opposed to the dark bitterness of his soul is marked the gentleness and straightforwardness of Duncan. Opposed to his moral weakness is seen the strength of his wife. Yet she, who is so brave in the beginning, loses her courage in the end. "A little water will clear us of this deed," confidently says Lady Macbeth after the murder of her guest; yet later in her sleep she moans, "All the perfumes of Arabia will not sweeten this little hand." Macbeth, she has once scornfully remarked, is not likely to achieve his kingly ambitions because his nature has been weakened by the "milk of human kindness." Yet on his last field of battle, when, on inquiry, Seyton informs him that a noise heard is the cry of terrorstricken women in the castle, the hero remarks quite calmly:

> I have almost forgot the taste of fears:
> The time has been, my senses would have cool'd
> To hear a night-shriek; and my fell of hair
> Would at a dismal treatise rouse and stir
> As life were in 't: I have supp'd full with horrors;
> Direness, familiar to my slaughterous thoughts,
> Cannot once start me.

What greater contrast could any audience ask than that provided by the coarse humor of the Porter's lines following immediately on the dark moments of Duncan's murder; or the recurring appearance of the shrieking witches and the silent ghosts between the scenes of more natural human action?

If one opens the covers of a modern play, one finds the same broad contrasts marked. In Ibsen's *A Doll's House* there is the conflict between the different ideals of the imaginative Nora and the stolid Torvald; the variation between the two aspects of the heroine's character observed at the beginning and at the end; the opposing qualities, similarly shown on different levels, between the characters of Mrs. Linde, Krogstad, and Dr. Rank, and then again between all the secondary characters and the leading ones—and so on. The juxtaposition of the scenes depicting Nora's relationship to her children with the scenes showing the development of Krogstad's threat is typical of Ibsen's story-telling technique. A moment's thought given to any of Ibsen's other dramas—*Brand, An Enemy of the People, Hedda Gabler, The Master Builder*—will convince one of the fondness which the "father of modern drama" had for theatric form of a strongly antithetical nature. His literary companions have not in any way spurned his methods. Consider the sex battles in Strindberg's *The Father* and *Countess Julie*; the social conflicts in Galsworthy's *Strife* and *Justice*; and the wars of spiritual adjustment in O'Neill's *The Hairy Ape* and *The Great God Brown*. Consider the characters which have been created to represent the opposing forces in these plays; and then consider the plots, made up most skillfully of scene and counterscene, speech and counterspeech, movement and countermovement, which have been built to shape all these parts into significant form. Sometimes the leading contrasts in drama are strongly pronounced, as in the plays just indicated. Sometimes they are extremely subtle, as in Anton Chekov's *The Cherry Orchard*. But they are always there, for any high-lighted story of life must contain them.

Visually and auditively expressed, contrast lies beneath all the effective differences between character and character, as well as between various phases of each character within himself. Prince Hal is distinct from Hotspur, Ophelia from the Queen. Hamlet is moody and abrupt; bitterly ironical, yet deeply tender; both affectionate and cruel. Nora is at different times doll and woman. All these tremendously important details must be brought out in the player's actions and voice tones, point being played against point until all is clear—until it is not only clear but emotionally exciting.

PRACTICAL
APPLICATIONS OF CONTRAST

Everything said with regard to the place of contrast in dramatic design is fairly obvious—when it is read on a printed page. Yet the principle here described is constantly ignored in practical design. Time after time we see on the professional, but chiefly the amateur, stage the deadly effects of sameness. The actors look alike; they all sound alike. There is no development in the panto-mime of the single actor, no change in the character of the group movements as a whole. Everyone talks at the same

rate of speed, never varying by more than a note or two
the median pitch and intensity of his voice. There is no
variety in the lighting. The actors blend with the scenery
and with each other. Everything is flat.

But there is no need for this monotony. The able director knows how to avoid it. Exploiting the factors of
space, time, and force, he works for the greatest possible
variety within each actor's pantomime. He contrasts
movement with movement and, whenever possible, shifts
around the whole plan of the player's action. While he is
working through visual contrasts to show the changing
thoughts and feelings within one stage personality, he is
likewise working for the differences between this character and the others with whom he comes in contact and
to whom he responds.

But it is not simply the form of the pantomime which
has to be considered. Its relationship to its setting must
also be planned. The actor must be dressed, made up,
lighted, and placed on the stage in such a way as to be
differentiated from his background. A position far upstage, or in a corner in the dark and next to a wall painted
in colors similar to those of the player's clothes and complexion, is manifestly a poor place for a character whose
facial and bodily expressions are important to the scene.

It is true that a particular moment of action, or a certain kind of role, may require the conduct just now indicated as that to be avoided. A lesser actor, for instance,
may purposely be placed in the shadow when the scene
involves more important characters, in order to keep his
presence minor. A lazy character may be required to
slouch. If his slouching presence must be made con-

actor and scenery—color

actor and scenery—shape

actor and actor—appearance

actor and actor—attitude

**THE CONTRAST OF ACTOR WITH SCENERY AND OF ACTOR WITH
ACTOR**

Four common devices for making an actor stand out on the stage. See
also the illustration on page 256.

spicuous, however, something may have to be done with
the position of the furniture he uses in order to have his
appearance stand out to the right degree. Usually, the
actor is directed to avoid identifying himself with furniture. Slumping on tables and burying himself in chairs
tends to make of him an environmental rather than a
central influence in the scene.

The actor should be moved around to different parts
of the stage. If the character impersonated is "quiet" or
"lazy," and the director for this reason wishes to avoid
having the actions of the actor appear in any way "nervous," he may have to prohibit all except the minimum of
action. Nevertheless, some little variation in the position
of a character (a leading one at any rate) is almost always
necessary for the appearance of naturalness, as well as for
the rounding out of expressiveness.

Characters are differentiated from each other by position and pose. If some characters sit, others may stand;
if some occupy one level, others may occupy another level.
The "operatic semicircle" and other all too perfectly sym-
metrical arrangements are usually undesirable.

One actor following another into the center of the
spectator's attention is usually placed by his director in a
different spot from the one occupied by his predecessor.
The director tries as far as practicability will allow to keep
the center of interest moving quietly or vigorously (depending on the play) around the acting area.

An important actor supposed to occupy forcefully the
center of attention is commonly dressed differently and
posed differently from the rest. He may be made simply

CONTRASTS IN THE DESIGNS OF GROUP SCENES

The use of contrasting lines, masses, and spacing in the formalized action of classical, musical, and other plays, as well as in the dance.

to stand while the others sit, or his head may be uncovered while the others have their hats on.

The director sets off an important entrance by making the stage for a moment unbalanced, or by forming in the stage picture a conspicuous hole which can be filled only by the entrance into it of the anticipated person.

Whenever the action permits, individuals are contrasted with groups, small groups with large ones. Contrasts in the action are made by the forming, dividing, and reforming of groups.

Devices of contrast similar to those in the visual field are employed in the auditive field. Each player uses a wide variety of voices, changing his pitch, volume, and tempo from passage to passage in order to bring out all the opposing values in his lines. The actors' median voices are differentiated from each other, particularly in pitch. This applies especially to long dialogue scenes. An important passage between two characters loses much of its essential "punch" if the voices speaking sound alike. Effective vocal composition depends on wise casting. A good director selects for his play not only sopranos and tenors, but some contraltos and basses; then he distributes these voices in such a way as to get the utmost out of the dramatic music. The recent New York production of Zoë Akins's *The Old Maid* seemed to me to fail conspicuously with regard to voice balancing. The play is chiefly about women. There is a sprinkling of men, mostly rather callow and juvenile. There is only one character who could be called thoroughly, substantially, maturely male, the doctor. In him should have been concentrated all the thundering bass qualities which were so sorely needed to give the play balance—and he was cast a tenor!

Some of the characters' voices must be contrasted with respect to inflectional patterns, force, and especially tempo. The youth must be differentiated from his father, the "city slicker" from the farmer, the woman of joy from the woman of sorrow, and so on. It is unnecessary to describe here all the devices which directors employ to work out the form of a stage design, for basically they are the same as those which operate in choral music. The forms available include, as we have already noted, solos, duets, trios, quartets, and mass passages, all of which can be developed only through a free use of contrast.

CONTRASTS BETWEEN SCENES

The composition of scenes is as important to the total design of dance and song as is the composition of elements within scenes. The several large sections of action must be viewed by the director as component parts of a greater whole, and must be shaped and fitted and developed through contrast in exactly the same way as the smallest details. Any weakness here spells the failure of the play.

Before he lays out the major lines of the stage composition, the director should study the play script carefully. In it he will usually find clearly indicated many of the points where the general changes of movement, pitch, and tempo should occur. One will find such stage directions as "The old people hobble out, and four little boys run on to the scene"; "The voices of the two men, friendly a moment ago, now begin to rise in anger"; or "A hush falls over the company." These leave the director in very little doubt as to what should be done. But a playwright never points out all the places where changes should occur; many must be determined by the sense of the director. If he is alert to the need for variation, he can usually find these spots without difficulty. There is a sequence, perhaps, in which two long, somewhat static conversational passages are divided by a short scene in which a neighbor or some children come in. The playwright, we assume, gives very little in the way of directions for this interruption. Taken by itself, the scene might be interpreted in a number of different ways—slow or quick, lively or subdued, noisy or quiet. When the director considers the scene in its line of sequence, however, he will quickly see that the interrupting scene should be positively active. After the first long conversation, the stage cries out for some kind of pantomimic and vocal freshening before it settles down for the next quiet scene.

The night, they say, seems darkest just before the dawn. That is an illusion governed by natural laws. A similar effect of opposition between dark and light—or up and down, or near and far—appears time and again in all successful dramatic performances. The difference between the natural and the theatric designs which produce these effects of heightened changes lies in the fact that, while the blackness in a natural night really remains the

same, the blackness in the dramatic plan may be artificially
deepened just before the turn. The darker the stage night
really is just before the dawn, the brighter will *seem* to
be the flood of light. The principle behind this illusion
is called the "law of effective contrast," and it is used, not
only in the theatre, but, of course, in every other field of
art. The quality of an oblique line in a drawing is accentuated when next to it is placed a horizontal or vertical
line; a tall figure in a painting seems markedly tall if next
to it is placed an extra-short figure; a spot of orange gains
brilliance when its complement, blue, is put beside it;
consonances in music sound doubly sweet when they follow dissonances.

Shakespeare, as a playwright, is a master artist in his
use of effective contrast. Over and over again he uses
short comedy scenes to heighten the effect of tragic scenes
preceding and still more tragic scenes to follow. The moment of greatest hope comes before the final despair, or
all is made to seem lost just before the upward turn in
fortune. Every skillful author uses this device to point the
high, or low, moments in his action; and it should be the
purpose of the director to spot the points where they
occur and guide his players into a clear translation of
them. Where the contrasts in pantomimic and vocal delivery may most logically and effectively be employed is
not, as we have said, always specifically stated in the
script. Sometimes the author does not fully recognize
them himself. At such times the director performs one
of his most important functions as an artist.

The attitude toward stage design here described is, of
course, primarily "theatrical." However, the artist-play-

maker commonly finds that theatrical advisability and
dramatic necessity walk together. The director who, con-
fronted with the problem of planning Act I of A *Doll's
House,* failed to work out enough lively action for the
happy moment between Nora and her children discovered
that the following tight conversation with the threaten-
ing Krogstad somehow lacked bite.

PRINCIPLES OF ORDER:
UNITY

Contrasting values are employed by the artist to *build up*
a design—to point out the high by comparing it with the
low, to show the strong by indicating the weak, to make
clear how different are the opposing forces of the play.
But all these contrasting details in the picture have very
little final meaning if they do not "hang together." Effective design has often been defined as "unity in variety."

The most far-reaching emotions in the theatre spring
from moods. To maintain their force, they must be fed
by impressions all, as it were, traveling along together in
the same direction. Unrelated, wrongly pointed stimuli
are distracting. Unity seizes on certain contrasts, with all
their contributing factors, binds them within a limited
enclosure where, from a single point of view and within a
single period of time, they may be observed to advantage.
It shapes and relates them so that they become kin, and
produces from them all the master effect described at the

UNITY IN THE SCENE

Three of many devices for making stage unity. Because the figures of the players must be shown small, the methods can be illustrated here only rather crudely. The center of interest in an actual scene may be established without the help of a raised platform, and the common-element type of unity without such obvious properties as round hats and tambourines. The unifying elements may be very subtle: related line or color notes in the costumes, or similar details of attitude and gesture in the action.

beginning of the chapter. Unity removes every element that cannot be made to contribute to this effect, and so ensures the maximum of intellectual and sensuous pleasure that may be served up to the banqueter, one might say, in a single dish at a single sitting.

There is nothing which more powerfully makes for unity than the early establishment of just one point of view for the play. The director makes all the scenes point in one direction, a direction which is in line with the primary drive of the central character. The prince wants the throne, the young wife wants to establish the freedom of her conscience, the group of poor weavers wants to better its economic condition, Mrs. Jones wants to marry off her daughter. Everything seen or heard on the stage is somehow related to one wish. Where there is a single point of view, there are bound to be certain common elements running throughout. This is the basis of *harmony*, one phase of unity. Whenever two or more characters share at the same point a similarity of idea, or a certain likeness of behavior, at that point a state of effective harmony is established between them. The same kind of tie makes different scenes follow each other in harmonic sequence. The greater the impressive strength of the common elements running through the several parts of the design, the greater is the harmony.

No play of Shakespeare contains more clearly marked contrasts in character than *King Henry IV, Part One*. But the varied personalities of this play, with all their wide differences, are strongly banded together by certain common ties and nationality. *King Henry IV* is an entirely

ACTION

Two illustrations of action conceived as the pursuit of adjustment. The scenes depicted are obviously unfinished. The spectator anticipates in each scene something to come. From Fred Koch, Jr.'s *Those Doggone Elections*, and Josephina Niggli's *Tooth or Shave*, as produced by the Carolina Playmakers.

ACTIVE SCENERY

The diagonal elements create an active feeling in two classical settings which would otherwise appear somewhat static. Because the play acted in these environments is itself designed in a modern spirit, liberties were taken with the style of the scenery. From *The Defense of Xantippe*, by L. H. Morstin, produced at the Polish Theatre, Warsaw, 1939.

British play. It is not difficult to imagine how much unity would be lost if the dramatist had made Hal a Frenchman, say, Falstaff a German, or Gadshill, Peto, and Bardolph Italians. The individuality of Hotspur is compared at different points in the action with that of the flexible Hal, the tedious Glendower, the home-loving Lady Percy, and, by his own story, with a certain perfumed lordling. Each of the contrasts is sharply drawn; but in the comparison of this character with those of so many other people, none of his own singleness of nature is lost, because in each case the comparison is made in the field of *selected* qualities. Hamlet, Othello, and Lady Macbeth each possess a nature full of conflicts; yet none of the actions of these people seems to be improbable, for the many sides of character displayed by each have all the same core. An even more consequential use of the common-quality device for character synthesis may be observed in the modern play already mentioned, *The Cherry Orchard*. The different phases of feeling and action here are so closely united by similar national, class, and family traits that the contrasts can be drawn only very delicately.

Guarding the center of interest is another aid to unity. What is dramatically the most important action in each scene must always have the first interest of the spectator. The experienced director is ever on the lookout for that common tendency of some players to indulge in the fidgets or a little horseplay on the side when they should be concentrating on another's speech or pantomime. This is not to say that there should never be any incidental action; sometimes such action is necessary to make the scene as

a whole seem natural and understandable. But, whatever
the side action is, it should be related to the central point
of movement, and should feed it, even if indirectly.

There should be a continuous line of connection between all the moments of a play from beginning to end.
Nothing should ever take the audience completely by
surprise. It is perfectly right, of course, to let a scene of
quiet action be stopped suddenly by the entrance of a
messenger, to let a period of comparative silence be
broken by a shout. But the quality of unexpectedness in
each change of movement and sound should be more
apparent than real. Beneath the half-startled reaction of
the spectator should be a feeling which, if it were expressed
in words, would say, "I had a hunch something like this
was coming!" A good example of failure to regard this important principle of interrelationship between points of
contrast was a courtroom scene enacted on an amateur
stage not long ago. A witness for the prosecution was being examined in a very humdrum sort of way. There was
no tension in the air. Suddenly, the father of the defend-
ant, who had been sitting quietly by, rose and fired a
bullet at the opposing attorney. The effect was awakening, to say the least. It stirred the audience; but not, unfortunately, in a very satisfactory way. There was no underlying preparation for that shot, and, consequently, the
audience felt cheated. The moment of noise, exciting as
it was, had no apparent connection with the main action
of the scene. It was an "effect," and nothing else. While
the audience was recovering, emotionally and intellectually, from the unforeshadowed shock, the following
action was confused or lost. The fault lay, of course, with

TRANSITION AS A UNIFYING DEVICE

For the purpose of unity, the opposing elements in a contrast arrangement may be tied together by a transitional line or shape or by a transitional color. Shown here are some common transitions in everyday design: the decorative spot which carries the eye round the corner of a frame or border; the cornice molding which binds the ceiling line to the wall; the foliage which ties a tower to the earth; the collar which unifies a shoulder line with the neck. The gray hill in the last drawing serves as an intermediary value between the blackness of the foreground and the lightness of the background. In musical design, the modulation between contrasting keys is a transition.

TRANSITION ON THE STAGE

An intermediary figure, group, color, or element of scenery may serve
to unite two contrasting persons or masses of people. The man on his
knees softens the opposition between the vertical and the horizontal
figures. The man standing hesitantly at the base of the steps is a con-
necting link between the two antagonistic groups. The figures in gray
unite the woman in black with the men and women in white.

the building of the scene before the shot. Quietness of movement and quietness of tone were needed to point the change about to take place; but the quietness should have been forced, showing the growing uneasiness of everyone in the courtroom. Then, when the shot came, it would have affected the audience like the electric thunder-roar which suddenly breaks from an overcharged cloud, instead of being just a clap of noise.

Style provides potent influence for unity. For instance, the only way in which all the different free elements of farce and poetry in a play like Shakespeare's *The Taming of the Shrew* can be satisfactorily tied together is by giving respect to the author's evident intention to have the action from beginning to end carried out in caricature, somewhat in the manner of puppets. This element of style is an all-important one, and many experienced directors fail to recognize it. The presentation of *The Emperor Jones* calls for a distinct mode, one related throughout to the superstitious beating of a drum. Other plays require other styles, naturalistic, formal, romantic, serious, or comic. *Sun-up, Antigone, The Romancers, Macbeth, You Can't Take It with You,* each must have its own mode, and the director who fails to establish and maintain the right one forfeits all hope for unity in his play design.

PRINCIPLES OF ORDER:
PHRASING

The natural disposition of the human mind to group sense impressions into rhythmic patterns has been brought out earlier in the book. Rhythmic grouping, it was noted, favors perception; it also adjusts the strain of attention. In poetry and music, in well-planned paintings, sculpture, and architectural designs, the rhythmic order helps us to grasp the magnitude of the units which we wish to contemplate. Thus we are enabled to adjust the effort of our attention in such a way as to seize the unit at the strategic moment, and then to relax for a moment before passing on to the next unit. Human attention is naturally periodic. It flows, not in a steady stream, but by jets. The most successful designs, whether they be in speech, in music, or in the visual arts, are set off into periods in such a way as to exploit to the fullest possible extent the pulsations in the observer's attention.

Because designed rhythm gives the listener or the seer a sort of biological device with which to sense out the underlying character of a composition and the direction in which the related accents are marching, he is able to project his feelings beyond his immediate impressions and estimate the larger form. Having grasped the pattern of the smaller groupings, he reaches out to grasp the more extensive ones—the groupings of groupings. Thus, rhythm adds to perception the values of perspective and expectancy—two of the most important factors in one's response to design.

The rhythmical grouping of impressions, whether visual, aural, or connected with any other sense, is called phrasing. Says Douglas Moore in *Listening to Music:* "Our minds cannot comprehend any succession of stimuli without an occasional instant of repose. If the stimuli engaging our attention do not provide a break so that the whole divides itself into fragments which we can assimilate, one of two things happens; either we cease to pay attention or we break them up ourselves. . . . Phrasing is as necessary in music as in poetry because our limited powers of attention demand it. If you will observe any piece of music that you hear, no matter how long, you will see that it is made up of a succession of phrases." [2]

The principle assigned here to music and connected, by reference, to poetry, applies with special force to the projection of stage dialogue and movement. When a dramatic scene is expertly directed and played, the rhythmical grouping is readily observable first in the acting unit formed roughly around the single "speech," and then, in a larger and more important aspect, in the group of units which fill out a movement of thought or feeling. A long speech, like a soliloquy in Shakespeare or an address in a modern play, may constitute a whole period in itself, and it may be made up of several unit phrases, separated by pauses, and set off from each other by changes in pitch, time, and force. Consider, for example, a rendering of the following address by Washington to his men in Maxwell Anderson's *Valley Forge.*

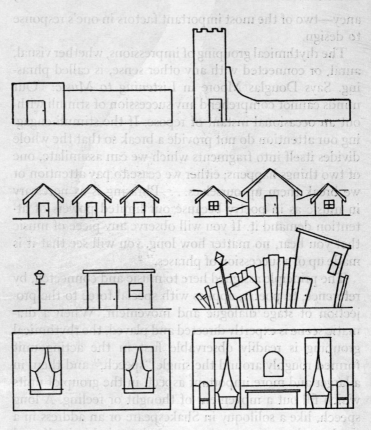

CONTRAST AND UNITY IN SCENERY DESIGN

These drawings show how weak, monotonous scenery may be made
more dramatically interesting through the use of contrasts held together
by transitions, and by other unifying elements.

Brett Weston

CONTRAST MAKES FORM

Contrast seen as an opposition of values. Without the light and shadow, the sand dune would be visually formless. *Oceano Dune.*

CONTRAST MAKES FORM

Contrast seen as an opposition of forces. If the two fighters were not driving against each other, the scene represented by this lithograph would be dramatically formless. A *Stag at Sharkey's,* by George Bellows.

Well, Master Teague, if they catch you they'll give seventy-five lashes, and that's a good deal to take and live./ On the other hand you're quite right from your own angle, and if I were you I'd feel as you do./—But this you should know, sir: if you go home, and we all go home this winter, you won't need to bother about coming back in the spring. There'll be no fighting to come back to.—General Howe will march out of Philadelphia and take over these states of ours./ If he knew now how many had deserted, how many are sick, how many unfit for duty on account of the lack of food and clothes and munitions, he'd come out in force and wring our necks one by one, and the neck of our sickly little revolution along with us./ So far we've kept him pinned in Philadelphia by sheer bluster and bluff and show of arms. We've raided his supplies and cut off his shipping and captured his food-trains and so bedeviled him generally that he thinks there's still an army here./ But every able-bodied man, every man that owns a pair of dungarees for his legs and brogans for his feet, has to look like ten men if this nation's coming through the winter alive./—What are we in this war for? Are we tired of it? Do we want to quit? [3]

One can imagine what an experienced actor would do with this passage. He would doubtless break it up into parts approximating those set off by the diagonal marks (/), and contrast the sections, or phrases, by the use of the vocal changes suggested in Chapter Four. He might drop his voice or raise it slightly, increase or retard his pace, or alter the volume. Thus he would help the listener to grasp the meaning.

If a single long speech, like the one just quoted, constitutes in itself several phrase units, rapid dialogue, on the other hand, may have to be grouped in such a way as

to include several short speeches in each division. The
phrasing of pantomime is similar. Sometimes several
phrases are required to complete a single sequence of
movements by one actor. Sometimes—as is usual in fast
farce action—the phrase group will cover the movements
of several actors working together to complete a single
pattern.

The method of phrasing a dialogue passage may be
illustrated in the opening scene from *The House of Con-*

CONTRAST AND UNITY IN SCENERY DESIGN

Scenery improved by a respacing of mass elements and a development
of the light and dark values.

nelly (quoted on pages 58–60). The first four speeches
(with their accompanying movements) constitute a unit
of feeling around the idea of "Poor Purvis!" The next four
touch on the idea of blood relationship, and so they are
grouped together. Then there is a sequence of three
speeches springing out of the memory of the hanging. Each
of these groups, swinging out of the underlying rhythm of
the scene taken as a whole, is a phrase division and should
be sensed (consciously or unconsciously) as such by the
actor. The gun is fired. The two old Negro women pause
a moment to notice it, then go back to their digging and
chanting. Soon the gun is fired again. Then, after a few

more speeches, the girl Patsy enters. These points mark the larger divisions.

If this scene were well played, the audience listening and watching probably would not once think the word "phrase." If the average spectator should be asked how the speech and movement had been arranged, he would be unable to recall noticing a single specific rhythmical feature. Yet he would have *felt* the rhythm; and because the scene had been carefully phrased, with due attention to pause and accent, he would long remember the scene as being emotionally effective.

The grouping of impressions into phrases is never governed (except, perhaps, in certain classical musical forms) by any rules. Successful phrasing is accomplished by feeling, not by mathematics. The rhythmic elements are very free, and they vary, of course, with the changing character of the design taken as a whole. The divisions between phrases may be marked by clean-cut pauses. Often there is only a slight lessening of tension, without any clean break at all. But even this moment of repose serves to rest the attention of the spectator and help him to gather up his forces of response for the next unit coming.

PRINCIPLES OF ORDER: SURGE

Every effective dramatic composition has an orderly beginning, middle, and end. The rhythmical action progresses logically from phrase to phrase and thence to the larger periods. But the action does not travel in a perfectly straight line. It undulates. The emotions of the characters in the play, aroused and driven through conflict, surge like the waves of the sea, bringing to certain points of the action a power not possessed by others. There are small peaks of intensified action and larger peaks of the same action, all leading rhythmically up and up to the great culminating peak of the scene, and then of the play. At this point in the action (if it has been well handled) the feeling of the audience which has been following the progress of movement reaches its highest pitch. The final surge of activity which stimulates this greatest flow of emotion is called, of course, the "major climax." The strongest surges, identified with the "most thrilling moments" of the scene, or play, are very easily recognized. But inexperienced actors and directors commonly miss the minor surges.

The following excerpt, taken from Paul Green's one-act play *Fixin's*, illustrates the lesser climaxes in dramatic action, and provides a hint as to how the actor, guided by the director, should use those forms in his performance. Lilly Robinson, who has been away for a few days visiting in a near-by town, has just returned to her home. A neighbor has gossiped in her absence, and her husband is in an unhappy mood.

(*As she enters,* ED *begins lacing up his shoes and putting his overall jacket on again. He does not look at her after the first glance of recognition.* LILLY *stands, undecided, in the doorway, waits an instant, then moves into the room, closing the door behind her.*)

LILLY: Ed, I was sorter expecting you to meet me. (ED *makes no reply, but picks up his clothes and carries them back to the room at the left.* LILLY *watches him uncertainly.*) Was you going somewheres, Ed?

ED: (*Reappearing*) No, not now.

LILLY: (*Dropping her suitcase on the floor and standing, undecided.*) Ed . . . I didn't mean to stay an extry week . . . but I wrote you why I wanted to. You got my letter; didn't you?

ED: (*Glumly*) No, I hain't heard a word from you. (*Picking up the dishcloth and moving to the stove.*) But I've heerd *about* you.

LILLY: What, what have you heard?

ED: (*Dully*) Have off yer things, and make yerself at home.

LILLY: (*Mechanically pulling off her coat and hat and laying them on the table.*) What'n the world ails you, Ed? You ain't mad about something, are you?

ED: I reckon I'm not.

LILLY: I wrote to you, Ed, and I told you to meet me in Angier this evenin'. If it hadn't been for Mr. Jake Turlington coming this way, I don't know how I'd 'a' got home.

ED: (*After a pause*) I ain't had no letter from you.

LILLY: I give it to Mr. . . . Mr. . . . Ryalls to mail for me. (*Thinking.*) No, I declare, I plumb forgot to mail it. It's lying on the bureau at Aunt Margaret's.

ED: (*A hard note slipping into his voice.*) Who is Mr. Ryalls?

LILLY: He was just a man who boarded there at Aunt Margaret's. I got acquainted with him over there.

ED: (*Turning to look her full in the face for a moment.*) How *well* did you get acquainted?

LILLY: (*In surprise.*) I . . . I don't know just what you mean.

ED: He don't happen to be a fellow you knowed last spring when you was over there, does he?

LILLY: Why, no, I never saw him before this time. And . . . he . . . he was pretty nice to May Belle—

ED: And how about you?

LILLY: Well . . . why he treated me all right.

ED: (*Suddenly flaring out.*) By God, I reckon he did! (*And he goes on with his cooking.*)

LILLY: (*Startled.*) Ed, what you so upset about? You said you'd heard about me. What . . . what have you heard?

ED: I reckon you been enjoying yerself all right.

LILLY: (*Dubiously*) Yes, I sure have. (*Turning quickly to him.*) What's all this you're driving at?

ED: Nothing. (*After a moment.*) Looks like you could help me get a little supper—if you ain't above it. (*She leans against the table a moment, looking at her hands. Her brow is wrinkled in thought. Suddenly she looks up at his broad back with a touch of fear in her face.*)

LILLY: Oh, what am I thinking about.—Here, you set down and let me fix for you. My goodness, you've burnt your meat slam to pieces! (*She bustles around the stove, putting in wood, cutting meat, and straightening the table, laying out dishes, etc. Ed sticks the dishcloth towards her, sits down in a chair and begins drumming on the table.*) How have you been getting along?

ED: Oh, purty good. How's Aunt Margaret and all of 'em over there?

LILLY: All right. (*Fumbling in the cupboard.*) Cain't we have some eggs? (*Ed makes no reply.*) Oh, here they are. My, my, the hens must have been a-laying! Must 'a' tuk a notion and started in all of a sudden. Ain't been eating many of 'em, have you?

ED: (*Beginning to whistle a low meaningless tune and tapping with his fingers on the table.*) No, not many. (*He goes on whistling. LILLY *turns from her work now and then to glance at him. Her quickening movements show her nervous perturbation. She goes on talking.*)

LILLY: Has the little white pullet we set come off yet? She was to come off sometime this week.

ED: (*Mechanically*) Uh huh. (*He continues whistling and tapping.*)

LILLY: (*Begins breaking the eggs into a dish.*) How many eggs did she hatch? You know we put twelve under her. (ED *makes no reply, his eyes narrowing to slits and his jaw taking on a more and more firm look. His whistle is more pronounced and the tapping on the table sharper and more staccato. As* LILLY *moves around the table, she crunches a piece of the broken vase underfoot. Suddenly she stoops, finds the remains of the vase and flowers, and with an exclamation of pain and hurt, she gathers them up. She turns sharply toward* ED *with a defiant and bitter word on her lips, but his inner absorption deters her for a moment. Tears of anger glisten in her eyes. She stirs the eggs more and more rapidly. At last with a stifled sob she whirls upon him.*) Who ... who broke my purty blue vase? (*He makes no answer. She bursts out more shrilly.*) Ed Robinson, I want to know who broke my vase?

ED: (*Suddenly bringing his fist down on the table in a shattering blow and roaring out his words in a rage*) Damn it to hell, I want to know what you been doin' with that Ryalls fellow over there at Dunn?

LILLY: (*Laying the remnants of the vase on the table and backing away from him*) I ... I ain't been doing nothing. What ... you ... mean?

ED: Yes, you have been doing something, or else ... (*She looks miserably into his face, his words dying away into a mutter. They both are silent a moment.* LILLY *twists the dried flowers in her hands.*)[4]

This scene would lose greatly in expressive values if it were played on a level—even if the individual speeches were shaped with vitality. There must be high places and low places because the emotions of the characters are in flux. There would doubtless be a minor surge where Lilly pulls off her hat and coat and, laying them on the table with a glance at her husband, asks: "What 'n the world ails you, Ed?" The tones and movements of the two remain on a level of intensity for two or three speeches, and then Ed suddenly asks: "Who is Mr. Ryalls?" The action now begins to rise, reaching a minor crest in the outburst of Ed, and Lilly's startled response. There is a momentary ebb. But when Ed refuses to answer Lilly's nervous question about the eggs and begins to whistle, the action starts to build again. In the following speeches the feelings rise rapidly. The highest point for this fragment of the play occurs where Lilly cries out shrilly about her vase and Ed crashes his fist on the table. In later scenes the emotions rise still higher, until Lilly walks out of the house. And there is a brief period of ebb before the curtain.

Dramatic climax is thus like the movement of the sea. The great swells (representing the primary surges) carry on their backs the larger waves and the smaller breakers (the secondary and still lesser surges). The crest of a rolling wave suggests the varying climaxes, or movements of top action. The edges of foam are the accents. All the climaxes, little and big, like the moving water, are ultimately related, of course, to the single flow of one dramatic tide.

It is surely unnecessary to point out that the phrasing

plan described in the preceding section is dependent on the movement of the dramatic surges described here. In fact, the two principles are practically united and might well be considered as one. Fundamentally, the rhythmical grouping designed to facilitate attention and perception is also the same kind of grouping as that which expresses the swinging changes in the emotions.

Many problems of dramatic design can be solved by the experienced artist through the cool use of reason. Improvements in points of contrast and unity can often be *thought* out quite efficiently. Design by rhythm, however, cannot be intellectualized. The rhythmic impulses of the artist grow out of rhythmic action. Too much thinking tends to stop the pulse beats. This is especially true on the stage. No actor can give movement to his words and pantomime by concentrating deliberately on the time measures. Neither can the director. Rather, they must enter into the swinging thought and emotions of the characters to be portrayed, and let the "feelings" engendered serve as the chief prompter for the shape and time of the action. That is not for a moment to deny that careful thought will *intensify* and *develop* the design, but the spring of that design lies in impulse.

An intensive experience of the rhythms produced by other sensitive artists often helps to order the rhythmical urges behind one's own work. There is no method for developing the rhythmic sense better than actual dancing. Singing and playing a musical instrument are also helpful, but they cannot compare with dancing, for dancing exercises the whole body. If one can do none of these, one can at least practice simple movement around the room to the time of appropriate musical patterns played on a phonograph. Even listening, without overt movement, is often productive. Music is an especially effective teacher because the forms within it, though fixed, are compelling, and they represent widely different kinds of rhythm which one may feel out. Simple rhythms, compound rhythms, rhythms of rhythms, they are all in music.

DEVELOPING THE POINTS IN CHARACTER, STORY, AND COMMENT

On the basis of all that we have thus far said, one can draw up a summary showing some of the principal features of a "dramatic" performance.

1. The performance is dancelike and songlike. It is rhythmic and melodic.

2. The performance is active. It is designed: (a) with considerable movement in space; (b) with many changes in tonal and pantomimic values (the factors of time, space, pitch, and force being exploited freely); and (c) with the sense of expectancy kept constantly alive. (The audience feels through every moment of the play that important "adjustments" are impending.)

3. The performance is ordered for maximum effect. The player and the director develop both the smaller and the larger elements of the composition with *contrast*, controlled by *unity*. They phrase speech and movement into rhythmical units, and surge these forward in wavelike

periods up and up to the culminating action peaks. A truly dramatic performance is marked by flow and ebb. Ebb prepares for flow, and where there is the greatest flow, there, of course, is the most exciting moment of the play.

But, needless to say, all this technique alone does not make drama. It serves simply to build up the vehicle. In the opening chapter we suggested that an audience comes to the theatre looking for three things: interesting characters in an interesting story, and some pungent comment on the action portrayed. The kind of performance we have been describing in this book is the means for projecting on the highest possible level those three elements which the audience desires.

All concepts of theatric design go back finally to the contemplation of human character. Drama begins and ends with this factor. Personality is both the cause and the result of all the searchings, conflicts, and resolutions which take place in every aspect of action between curtain rise and curtain fall. Effective characterization represents, consequently, the finest and most important achievement of the playwright, the actor, the director, and all the other artists of the stage.

Story, viewed as something aside from character, is plot. Considered in its simplest terms it is the pursuit of adjustment described in the last chapter. At the basis of every plot is the desire for something unfulfilled. But the path to the achievement of each satisfaction is blocked by a counterforce. Sometimes it is outward, sometimes inward. There are men who do not wish the nobleman to have the crown he covets; friends of the murdered man, or the prince's own indecision, stand in the path of revenge;

the misunderstanding of an unimaginative husband opposes the attempt of the young woman to establish her spiritual independence; a girl's obstinate fancy bars her lover's union with her. Then there is struggle. The keener the real or imagined lack of adjustment, and the keener the resulting desire and consequent struggle, the more exciting tends to be the story.

Comment, as we have seen, is represented by the philosophical remarks made by the playwright, and in turn by the performers, in and between the lines of the play. In the works of such a writer as Bernard Shaw, the philosophical comment is abundant and explicit. In the works of other thoughtful playwrights it is equally abundant, but more implicit—that is, it is *suggested* by the action, instead of being stated in words. *What Price Glory* is an example. Many plays which are strictly "entertainment" lack comment. Often they are successful in a popular sense; but critics and discriminating playgoers are disposed to label these pieces "sentimental," or "melodramatic," or "unmotivated." Even a little seasoning of philosophy seems to add immeasurably to the flavor of the drama. Generally speaking, the most popular as well as the more thoughtful audiences prefer to take the jam of sweet emotion like the filling of a sandwich, between two slices of intellectual bread.

What the director and the actor can do in order to guard and intensify the character, story, and philosophical values of a play can be clearly defined. First, they can analyze the story of a play carefully for the springs of action. These they will find, of course, in the motivating reach, or desire, of the leading character or characters, in

the influences which oppose the fulfillment of the adjustment, and in the impulses for battle natural to the frustration. (We are speaking, of course, of *typical* plays. A few
atmospheric plays and some pageantlike showpieces cannot be so satisfactorily analyzed in this way. But such
plays are rare.)

When the director puts the play on the stage, he will
work to bring out these points. He will strive to show in
the actions of the leading character (such as Hamlet) or
the leading characters (such as Romeo and Juliet) that
the forces of desire are keen, and in the behavior of those
elements which oppose the fulfillment of desire (the cor-
rupt court and Hamlet's hesitant nature, hatred between
rival families) that the forces of resistance are stiff. He will
take the struggle which grows out of this opposition of
forces and develop it to the limit of the playwright's design.

The character of the struggle will vary, of course, from
play to play. In one situation it may be a great industrial
battle (as in Galsworthy's *Strife*), in another, an heroic
search for the meaning of a man's existence (as in
O'Neill's *The Hairy Ape*), or in another little more than
a competitive effort of two or three bright people to show
the agility of their minds, perhaps merely to "outsmart"
each other in witty conversation (as in one of Noel Cow-
ard's comedies). But within the play's frame, whether
large or small, the sense of conflict must be vigorous.

It is the function of the director to see that the story is
moving forward every minute. When the action cannot
progress outwardly, it must continue inwardly. During the
periods of inner action, however, when the more violent

movements of the body and voice have to be curbed, the actor cannot be allowed to retire completely into himself. Because the spectator, as we have seen, is no mind reader and cannot, without definite guidance, feel his way inward to the emotions of the characters whom he is following, the actor must continue to provide outward symbols of the inner action—subtle motions, slight but expressive changes of posture and tone. Never for an instant can there be any complete relaxation of emotional energy; but the intensity of this energy changes from time to time. The director causes the action to surge in character with the feelings of the people in the different scenes, building the effects of these action surges slowly, patiently but determinedly, up to the great climaxes of the play.

All the signposts that indicate the direction in which the story is unfolding must be made perfectly clear. This means that the audience should be able to hear or see distinctly: (1) every first reference to an important person or fact (establishing the knowledge, for instance, that a key figure is called Jones, and that he has just returned to town); (2) points of action which explain later action (like the placement of a fateful document or gun in the drawer of a certain desk); (3) words or gestures which pivot major changes of thought and feeling (such as the quiet remark that releases a flood of anger, the glance which reveals a secret).

In order to prevent the audience from missing the places where the shifts occur, the director will often have to mark them by stress, pause, or other forms of emphasis. If the play being performed is a realistic piece, all this shaping will have to be done subtly, for recognition of a "trick" often produces on the audience a very chilling effect.

Always, let us repeat, the director will give his primary thought to character, for it is out of the characters that the story properly springs. It is only because dramatic personalities are individually and collectively what they are that there are desire, counterdesire, and the exciting actions of conflict. Whenever the director feels that the story is flattening out and that there is no drive in it, he should immediately go back to the men and women who motivate the story and examine them. He will doubtless find that the characterizations are flabby.

From first to last, the director should remember that the real player is seated in the audience. The spectator out there is ready and eager to participate in exciting events, all of which he knows are leading up to some kind of climactic emotional experience at the end of the evening. But he can follow these adventures of the body and spirit only through the manifest behavior of the figures on the stage, and consequently the quality and extent of his enjoyment depend on the efficiency with which those stage guides perform their function.

THE DIRECTOR AS ARTIST

The whole study of design principles is valueless unless the man who uses them *feels* them to be a part of himself. If he is fundamentally an artist, he will recognize each principle discussed as an old friend, a truth, the essential validity of which he has sensed long ago. He may never have put that particular feeling into words, but he has long ago apprehended it as a part of his seeing, hearing, and doing.

Creation, it has repeatedly been said, is primarily a matter of personality. The act of composing music, a painting, or a play is not something external. It is a part of the inward man himself. It springs from the internal processes of his mind and his body, affected by a certain individual state of aliveness which we call temperament. To investigate the roots of creative designing, therefore, one must examine the artist, not as a behaviorist, but as a man.

How would one describe the artist in this light? He is, clearly, a person of keen intellectual insight. He thinks incisively and logically, and maintains at all times a fine objective attitude toward his subject matter and his medium. But he possesses two capacities which differentiate him from men of brains in other fields. One capacity is his extraordinary susceptibility to sensory impressions. The other is his peculiar lust for living. These two capacities united make a man of restless action who is continuously engaged in the adventure of sensing things in terms of their dynamic elements, a man full of eagerness to extract, reorganize, and build up these elements into still more effective forms.

In his aggressive vigor, the artist is contrasted with the sensitive, but comparatively inexpressive, people of which the everyday world is filled. He not only feels, he *does*. The old conception of the musician, the painter, the playwright, as a pale lily subsisting on light salads in a secluded garret has long ago been discarded. The greatest artists of history were physically, as well as mentally, vital people. Bach, Beethoven, and Brahms were robust men. Michelangelo was noted for his bodily endurance. Leonardo da Vinci for his great strength. (It has been said that he could mount unbroken stallions and bend a horseshoe as if it were a coil of lead.) The photographs of nearly all the leading American painters, illustrators, cartoonists, and industrial designers today reveal men of rugged build. The Mexican, Diego Rivera, a leader of Western artists, who has been ranked by some critics as the greatest of them all, is a man of gargantuan size and appetites. His remarkable virility has in no way hindered the tender quality of his painting. Rather it has enhanced that tenderness.

Over against such men as these may be raised, of course, the names of a few important creators, like Chopin, who were invalids. But it can be said of them that, in spite of the physical limitations imposed by their illness, they lived intensively. The basic ingredient of productive genius is nervous energy. Occasionally this energy is discovered in weak, disease-ridden bodies; but much more often it is found in strong ones.

If the driving power of the artist in the field of music or painting depends on physical vitality, much more must it depend on this same vitality in the dynamic field of the theatre. Evidence points to this fact. The most successful playwrights are notoriously vigorous individuals. Some of them have spent at least a part of their careers as farmers, sailors, soldiers, even as baseball players. Equally vital individuals are the leading directors. Here lies the reason, perhaps, why proportionately fewer women succeed in the two professions mentioned. They possess insufficient stamina. Though keen and quick to sense out the effective relationships in the moment-by-moment elements of play design, they often lack the basic biological strength to feel out the larger relationships, those which reach, not through minutes, but through whole hours of time. To sense the tie between the words uttered quietly, the actions rendered softly, in one act with the tempestuous moment in a distant scene, to hold all parts in proportion, and to make all the elements surge up to the great climaxes, requires, not just intellect, but a neuromuscular energy possessed by few—few men as well as women.

All the greatest men and women of the stage have been vital people, full of the joy and power of life. Art, in the last analysis, is simply living stepped up to a peak, and, consequently, the people who create and interpret it have to be superpeople. Much of the contemporary theatre everywhere suffers woefully from the lack of simple biological vitality in the men and women who work in it.

Fortunately, vitality can be cultivated, at least to some extent; and it should be the purpose of every young designer-director to give primary attention to this phase of his development.

Chapter Seven

TECHNICAL ASPECTS OF THE DIRECTOR'S DESIGN

THE SPECIAL "RULES" OF THE STAGE

Complementing the general principles of composition which apply to painting, music, and other fields of art as well as to the theatre are several specific and very practical principles which hold strictly for the stage. Certain more or less mechanical arrangements have been found by directors over a long period of years, not necessarily to create effective dramatic form, but to help points of effective form to show themselves. Some established methods for securing clear lines of vision, for instance, have always been useful; so also have been certain methods for emphasizing the stature and enlarging the action of an

205

important figure. For the sake of convenience, these specialized principles of stage design are set down here as "rules"; but the reader should understand that most of them are merely statements of common practice. They must be regarded as tentative, relative, and adaptable to each new dramatic situation as it arises.

ELEMENTS OF VISUAL AND AUDITIVE DESIGN

Practical designing depends on a precise knowledge of one's media. The elements of stage design which the director must understand and learn to control are both visual and auditive. These two broad classifications may each, in turn, be subdivided into two others:

Visual elements: movements by actors
environmental shapes
Auditive elements: speech by actors
environmental sounds

The handling of the actors' movements will be considered first.

TWO FUNDAMENTAL "RULES" OF VISUAL DESIGN

Eyes are the point of departure for all visual design in the theatre, the eyes of the observer and the eyes of the actor.

COMPOSITION TO DIRECT THE SPECTATOR'S ATTENTION

The attention in this scene goes, first, to the figure on the landing because he is raised; then, to the figure in the lower left corner because (1) he is active, (2) the others are looking at him. From *Thunder Rock*, by Robert Ardley, produced by the Group Theatre.

COMPOSITION TO DIRECT THE SPECTATOR'S ATTENTION

The interest of the audience is directed to a spot at the rear of the scene because the faces of all the actors are turned that way. From the all-Negro version of *Macbeth*, produced by the WPA Federal Theatre Project of New York.

Lines of vision must be good, both on the stage and in the audience. The director cannot go very far wrong in his first steps of design if he remembers two fundamental "rules":

1. Keep the human presences on the stage in contact with each other through their eyes.

2. Keep the active faces, as much of the time as possible, in easy view of the audience.

The director finds the problem of fulfilling these two "rules" simplified when he imagines two basic eye lines, one on the stage, and one from the audience to the stage.

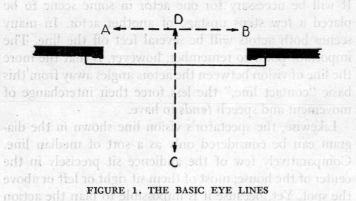

FIGURE 1. THE BASIC EYE LINES

The first line, indicated in the drawing above as A–B, is the actor's contact line. It extends across the stage, right and left, parallel to the proscenium and just far enough behind the curtain line to permit actors standing upon it to have their faces well illuminated by the stage lights. Human presences on the stage are shown in dramatic contact with each other when the lines of vision between them are related to this basic eye line, A–B.

The second line, indicated in the drawing by *C–D*, is the spectator's vision line. Ideally, it extends from the center of the house to the stage, at right angles to *A–B*. The active faces on the stage are seen by the audience when the direction of the eyes in those faces is related to this second basic line.

The word *basic* is used in each case advisedly because the director only starts his planning from these lines. For purposes of effective design, it would clearly be wrong to have all actors who are talking to each other in an important scene stand and face each other on the line *A–B*. It will be necessary for one actor in some scene to be placed a few steps upstage of another actor. In many scenes both actors will be several feet off the line. The important point to remember, however, is that the more the line of vision between the actors angles away from this basic "contact line," the less force their interchange of movement and speech *tends* to have.

Likewise, the spectator's vision line shown in the diagram can be considered only as a sort of median line. Comparatively few of the audience sit precisely in the center of the house; most of them sit right or left or above the spot. Yet, because it is impossible to plan the action on the stage so that it will be exactly right for the sight lines of everyone in the audience, the director finds it advisable to consider first what the people see who sit in the middle. When he designs his action so that the eyes of the leading dramatic actor are, in moments when they count most, clearly visible to a man seated in the ideal center, he knows that those eyes will be visible to more people in the house than if the action is designed primarily for a right- or left-angle sight line.

The fact that the line C–D runs straight to the stage does not mean, of course, that even the spectator who sits in the ideal center always sees the actors straight ahead of him. They will frequently be to the right or the left. The point the director remembers is simply that this is a basic guide line, and that the eyes of an actor are visible to the audience when the direction of his face is related to this line.

In the drawing (Figure 1), the lines representing the actor's basic contact line and the spectator's basic vision line are at right angles to each other. It is clearly impossible for an actor, however flexible his neck muscles may be, to look in the directions of A–B and C–D at one and the same time! What must he do? The answer is simply that he should work with the two. In his postures and actions from moment to moment he should indicate the influences exerted on him by each of the basic eye lines and maintain a dramatic balance between them.

FRACTIONAL FACES

But it is not necessary for an actor to face another actor, or to have his eyes visible to the audience, all the time. Practically, he may, in accordance with the situation, stand or sit with his face in any direction whatsoever— straight to the front, straight to the side, straight to the back, or at any angle between those points. Let us consider the actor's face at a few of the angles and see what characteristics may be noticed in each position.

The three-quarter-view angle is the most common one (Figure 2). Broadly speaking, when the faces of two actors in a scene are turned like this, halfway toward each

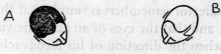

FIGURE 2. THE THREE-QUARTER VIEW OF THE ACTOR'S FACE

In this and the following figures A is the player referred to in the test, B his partner.

other, they may be said to be in their "normal" positions. The two influences, side and front, exerted by the two basic eye lines described above, are equal in these positions. The actors can easily look at each other, and the audience can clearly see their faces. We call these positions

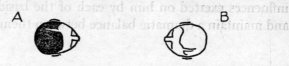

FIGURE 3. THE HALF, OR PROFILE, VIEW OF THE ACTOR'S FACE

"normal" simply because they are the positions commonly assumed by players at the beginning of a dialogue. And it is to these positions that they tend most frequently to return as the scene progresses. At the three-quarter-view angle, the players are usually engaged in a quiet form of interchange. They are talking together interestedly, but there is no urgent contact between them.

In moments of conflict, however, or when one character commands another, or when two characters observe each other searchingly, the eyes of the actors tend to meet straight-on (Figure 3). The half view, or profile, is characteristic, therefore, of tense action. In this position, the actors give and take directly into each other. The eye line of the audience is related to that vision line because the eyes of the actors can still be seen.

The face at the quarter-view angle is commonly used for two purposes: (1) to put variety into a scene (to

FIGURE 4. THE QUARTER VIEW OF THE ACTOR'S FACE

change the position of an actor, for instance, after he has been talking for some time straight across at the face of another actor); and (2) to throw the attention of the audience to the face of another actor. The face above (B in Figure 4) becomes in this action the more conspicuous because the spectator always tends to look at the face of which it can see most.

When the director must choose which of two faces on a diagonal contact line should be placed above, he naturally selects that which he considers dramatically more important at the moment. This face usually belongs to the leading character in the scene. Sometimes, however, it is attached to a minor one. It is not always easy, therefore, for the director to make distinctions. Let us imagine a scene from some play written around the exploits of Sherlock Holmes. A murder has been committed, and the great detective is interviewing the servants of the deceased in the sitting room. He may ask the pantry maid to sit on the sofa while he talks to her. In order to point

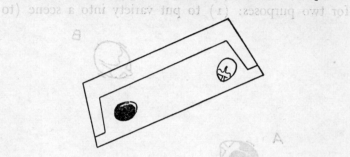

FIGURE 5. KEEP THE MORE ACTIVE FACE ABOVE

Sherlock Holmes is seated at the lower end of the couch, the pantry maid at the upper.

his question and force the answer from her, he sits on the sofa near her.

Which of these two characters should be placed above, which below? If the director feels that he is in a predicament, he should be able to derive some help from Rule 2 in the preceding section: "Keep the active faces in easy view of the audience." At the moment of this interview the more active face, presumably, is not the speaking face of the great detective (even though he may be the principal character in the scene), but the answering face of the little pantry maid. Therefore the director will place her at the upper end of the sofa and let her look down toward the audience (Figure 5). In this position, her changing expression will be in clear view of the audience, which will thus be enabled to judge for itself (as it will like to do) whether or not what she says in response to the probing questions is true. The audience is quite willing to forgo for the present the full sight of Holmes's face, because it

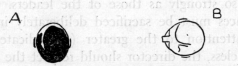

FIGURE 6. THE ACTOR'S FACE AWAY FROM THE AUDIENCE

can guess pretty well what expression is there, and will concentrate on the face of the pantry maid.

Occasionally the director will instruct an actor to turn his back to the audience and point his face straight upstage (Figure 6). This action is especially effective in certain moments of emotional stress when the expression of a character's eyes is better suggested than stated. An incident of this kind occurs in the first act of Philip Barry's *You and I*, when Nancy, troubled by the dark silence of her husband, offers him her comfort and affection and is answered, apparently without cause, by a curt remark. To hide her sudden pain, Nancy can turn her face away from Maitland's eyes toward the audience, but the effect is usually stronger when she turns her hurt into the privacy of the shadows at the back.

In some transitional movements between one stage

position and another, a leading actor will naturally turn his back on an audience. Contemplating all movements, however, which bring a principal's face straight upstage, or into the quarter-view angle described above, the director remembers that the actor's face is usually more valuable to the scene when the audience can see the eyes than when it cannot, and accordingly he does not keep the actor's face turned away for very long. The faces of the minor characters do not, of course, have to be considered so strongly as those of the leaders. Often the lesser faces must be sacrificed deliberately in order to throw attention to the greater (as indicated above). Nevertheless, the director should respect the audience's desire to see expression and keep as many active faces as possible, as much of the time as possible, in easy view of the audience.

THE FULL FACE
TO THE AUDIENCE

A good designer of stage action finds very little use for the full, straight-to-the-front face (Figure 7). It is true, of course, that when the player is turned this way the spectator can see him most completely. However, the player in a straight-front position is clearly violating Rule 1, for, looking straight into the eyes of the audience, he cannot possibly form any strong contact with his fellow actor.

Another thing which makes the full-front face unde-

sirable is the audience's sense of the "invisible fourth
wall." The spectator seeing the three walls of a room,
behind and to the sides of the actor, feels the presence
of another wall in front. He is uncomfortable, therefore,
when he sees a player apparently staring straight through
this wall. Even when delivering a "rostrum speech" (that
is, a speech to a stage audience, or a speech to the world
in general), or indulging in reverie, an actor should guard
against looking the audience directly in the eye. If he
angles his face only a few inches to the right or left, he
places himself back within the picture frame of the stage
and establishes once more the sense of reality.*

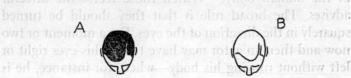

FIGURE 7. THE FULL FACE OF THE ACTOR TOWARD THE AUDIENCE

THE BODY
WITH THE FACE

The actor's body should be turned in the direction of his
eyes. The advisability of doing this is pretty obvious, yet

---

* In the stylized forms of vaudeville and opera, where contact between actor and actor and the illusion of the fourth wall is less important than a free relationship with the audience, players frequently
take the full-front attitude and keep it for considerable periods of time.
A certain amount of this kind of technique is often permissible also
in the performances of romantic and expressionistic plays.

it is frequently disregarded. On the amateur stage one so often sees the bodies of players planted in one position while their heads are twisted around in another. The straight-front mistake seems to be the greatest of the traps for untrained bodies. Over and over again one sees young players (and older ones, too) get caught here. In turning from a person on one side of the stage to one on the other side, they bring themselves around until they reach that magical straight-front position, where suddenly the body becomes locked and only the head moves on in the new direction. The two parts of the player are often so twisted away from each other that one marvels at the flexibility of the human body! "Watch those feet," the director advises. The broad rule is that they should be turned squarely in the direction of the eyes. For a moment or two now and then an actor may have to cast his eyes right or left without moving his body—when, for instance, he is standing between two persons in a compact group and is carrying on a conversation which includes both of them —but his feet, like Ruth in the Bible, should say to his eyes most of the time, "Wither thou goest, I will go."

THE BASIC CONTACT
LINE AND "STAGE CENTER"

In Figure 1, the basic line for contact between actors, A–B, is drawn downstage, close to the proscenium opening. The apprentice director reading these pages may wonder why the line is placed at this point and not up a few feet, through the center of the acting area. The reason is this: experience has shown that contacts between actor and actor usually are strongest when they are played out on a line close to the audience. A–B is a sort of foundation for the stage picture, and two persons within the proscenium frame tend to start the more important parts of their dialogue and movement on this line and return to it often as the scene progresses.

The magnetic center for the line, and for the stage as a whole, is the middle point in A–B. This spot, designated as "stage center," is the basic point of radiation and convergence for all movement in a scene.* To it and from it tends to flow the dramatic action. The normal position for two or three persons who are not otherwise attached is around this center.

As already suggested, the actor's basic contact line is not in quite the same position on every stage. It runs as close to the inner line of the proscenium as effective lighting will permit. Because overhead spotlights and border lights cannot be hung exactly alike on all stages—especially the makeshift type of community stage on which so many of us work—the director determines early just how far downstage his actors' faces can be seen to good advantage, and does not allow them to stand below this. For, without light, "basic contact" between characters means very little.

---

* Old-fashioned charts sometimes indicate a position halfway between the curtain line and the rear line of the acting area. Practically, however, the working center is below the actual middle of the floor space.

THE "DRAMATIC ANGLE"

When the forces of action and reaction in a scene are equally divided between two characters, the director brings them onto A–B, or a line parallel to it. In this position, as we have pointed out, the audience can see both faces with the same clarity, can observe the thrust and parry of the two sides with equal intensity, and is thus

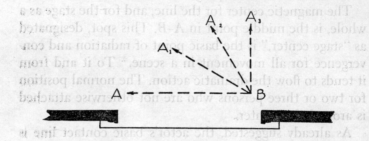

FIGURE 8. DRAMATIC AND UNDRAMATIC CONTACTS

enabled to feel out with the keenest possible interest the balance between them.

When the forces of action and reaction are unequal, the director usually puts one of the two actors upstage of the other. The upstage face naturally dominates the scene because it is in better view of the audience; so the director places upstage the character whose actions or reactions are more interesting. In the primary position, depicted in Figure 8, A shares interest with B. At the position A_1 he dominates B a little; at A_2 he forcefully dominates B; but there is a limit to this climb, for in the position A_3 the actor ceases to command any attention —he is hidden behind B.

Dramatic conflict is naturally felt to be at its greatest pitch when the forces of action and response on the two sides are equally matched. Broadly speaking, then, the interchange between two characters is strongest when they are arranged in the positions A–B, and the interchange tends to weaken the more the contact line between them angles away from the base. When they stand along the line A_3–B, the interchange ceases entirely, because the spectator can see none of it. We might set down another "rule," then: the more acute, or flat, is the angle between the actors' contact line and the basic contact line A–B, the more dramatic tends to be the action. The thrust and parry between A and B along the line A_1–B is almost as strong as it is along A–B. This cannot be said for the action along A_2–B.

One must not assume from this that the wide angle (meaning actors placed in positions A_2 and B) lacks value on the stage. There are many situations in which it is essential to the bringing out of some strong action or reaction on the part of one or the other of the two actors. It is important for the director to remember, however, that scenes of conflict, and other dramatic scenes in which an equal view of the two faces is desirable, are better played along the line A–B, or along a line forming an acute angle with it, than along a line which angles far away from A–B. Above all things let the director remember that the very wide angle has no value at all.*

* Unless A, in the upstage position, is standing on a higher level than B.

MOVING CHARACTERS APART
TO IMPROVE A CONTACT LINE

The director will frequently have to design a scene, usually of an introductory or transitional nature, in which it will seem necessary to keep one of the two equal characters downstage and the other upstage for some time.

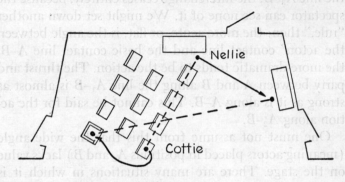

FIGURE 9. CHARACTERS MOVED APART TO IMPROVE THEIR LINE OF CONTACT

From *Cottie Mourns.*

The question arises, then, what the director should do about the principles of good angling just explained. A problem of this kind presented itself in a student production of Patricia McMullan's one-act play *Cottie Mourns.*[1] The center of the room had to be filled with chairs for a funeral, and provision made for entrances downstage on both sides. Because of the peculiar arrangement of furniture and doorways, it was necessary to open the play with Cottie near the footlights, and her companion, Nellie Merkel, away up by the rear wall.

The author, in her opening stage directions, describes the not overactive Cottie as sitting lazily in her favorite rocker while her more industrious friend arranges flowers on a table against the wall. Not willing to push Cottie upstage for fear of burying her in the mass of chairs, and unable to place Nellie Merkel down right or down left where the doorways were, the director put them in the positions indicated by the first dots in Figure 9. The contact line between the two figures through a rather long conversation was clearly bad. The play of comic mock grief on the face of the seated widow was very important to the scene, yet, whenever she turned to her friend, she hid her face from the audience. Nellie Merkel was likewise hidden from a full third of the audience because of her angle behind Cottie.

The arrangement of the scene was easily mended by having Cottie move her rocker to the end of the third line of seats at the right, and by having Nellie's table and vase shifted over to the left wall. It is true that in doing this the director had to increase the distance between the two women and leave the central part of the room bare of people (which is not usually very wise); but it is also true that when he moved the women to the new positions he turned a wide angle of interaction (the angle between the contact line of the two women and the basic contact line of the stage) into an acute angle, and so increased the dramatic effectiveness of the scene.

Of course, the director could not leave Cottie and Nellie Merkel at this one angle very long. Soon Cottie arose from her chair to quarrel with her friend, Nellie Merkel met her on a line in the center of the room, and the two women "went to it" in real earnest. Before Nellie was finally driven out the door at the right, the characters had used every part of the stage, with their faces first at one angle and then at another.

DIRECTING ATTENTION TO A CHARACTER IN A GROUP

The first rule in the composition of groups on the stage is to have always a single visual center of interest. The spectator can see only one thing at a time, and for this

FIGURE 10. DIRECTING ATTENTION TO A FIGURE UPSTAGE CENTER

reason he does not often favor in the theatre the three-ring plan of the circus. The center of interest should, of course, be the character (sometimes a group of characters

PICTURIZATION

Detail composition: an effective moment from Zoë Akins's dramatization of Edith Wharton's *The Old Maid*.

PICTURIZATION

Mass composition: a scene from *King Agis*, by Juljusz Stawacki, produced by the
National Theatre, Warsaw, 1928.

viewed as one personality) who at the moment is dramatically the most interesting. All the others on the stage
should feed the center of interest by making it a focal point
of attention. This usually means that they direct their eyes
to it. Several of the methods employed to lead the sight
of the audience to the dominant figure in a scene, through
the eye lines of the other characters, are indicated here.

FIGURE 11. DIRECTING ATTENTION TO A FIGURE UPSTAGE AT
THE SIDE

The easiest way to direct attention to a character is to
place him upstage at the apex of a triangle and have the
actors downstage of him turn their faces toward him
(Figure 10).

But the person to be accented does not necessarily have
to be in the middle of the group. From any position upstage he can command the attention if the other characters turn toward him (Figure 11).

Because the eyes of the audience tend to travel in the
direction in which most of the eyes on the stage are
turned, it is possible for the figure drawing attention to
be downstage of the group which is "feeding" him (Figure

12). If there were only two figures in this scene, one downstage and the other upstage, the attention of the spectator would naturally go to the face above. But because there are three figures here, and two are looking

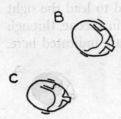

FIGURE 12. DIRECTING ATTENTION TO A FIGURE DOWNSTAGE AT THE SIDE

down to the one below, the attention goes to this downstage person.

The principles of composition which apply in this way to the arrangement of small groups of people on the stage apply with equal force to the arrangement of larger groups.

TAKING ATTENTION
AWAY FROM A CHARACTER

Instead of pointing attention to a character, it is sometimes necessary to draw attention from him. Usually, the simplest way to do this is to turn that character's face away from the audience. Another way is to move his face into a weak area—that is, somewhere away from the center of interest, preferably into the neutral shadows upstage or at the side of the stage. Great care must be taken to make the movement and final posture look easy and natural; otherwise the character will draw attention instead of passing out of it. Movement which contrasts strongly with the common action of a scene tends to be conspicuous. However, if the character turns quietly to look out the window or to warm himself at the fireplace, or walks over to glance at an interesting ornament or picture in the corner, the spectator will usually let him go without bothering about him.

Let us say again that the movement such a character makes must be consistent with himself and with the situation at large; otherwise it will not be successful. People do not hug fireplaces in the summertime; they do not gaze at pictures if they are naturally indifferent to pictures, or if their companions are discussing murder.

The director can ease the problem of withdrawing a character by maneuvering him around to the edge of the group before he is to be turned out of it. It is much easier to drop him off the side than to pluck him out of the center. And when the character takes his new position, he should be careful not to destroy its negative nature by holding himself too stiffly. The audience is likely to wonder why a man is studying and studying a picture, or holding his back stiffly to his companions for a time—and begin to watch him.

KEEPING THE ACTION BOUND IN

There is a common tendency for action in group scenes, unless it is carefully watched, to poke itself out at the audience in the center. That is, a character moves down toward the footlights in the middle of the stage and finds that the persons to whom he wishes to talk are upstage of

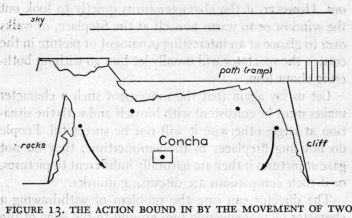

**FIGURE 13. THE ACTION BOUND IN BY THE MOVEMENT OF TWO
CHARACTERS DOWNSTAGE**
From *Soldadera*

him in the right and left corners. He is tempted then to turn his back on the audience so that he can see his companions; and, if he does respond to this temptation, he probably tangles the whole system of vision and contact lines which the director has been working out. The usual solution is to move the people at the sides also down toward the footlights. If the speaker in the center must maintain contact with only one of the side figures, he can stand on the base line, A–B, with him (Figure 1); but, if he must speak to characters to both the right and the left, he should stand a little above the base line where he can command both persons with his eyes.

Let us consider an example. At one point in the Carolina Playmakers' studio production of Josephina Niggli's *Soldadera,*[2] four soldier women stood upstage near a mountain path, talking about their leader, Concha. She made her appearance down this path, passed through the center of the group, and seated herself on a box by the campfire near the middle of the scene, several feet downstage of the women (Figure 13). She then began to speak to them. The student director of the play first considered the idea of having Concha sit with her back to the audience, but, deeming this inadvisable, she had the character turn straight to the front. The whole effect was very stiff and unnatural, because Concha seemed to be avoiding the eyes of her companions, when, as a matter of fact, she should have been seeking for them. The director finally brought downstage two of the soldier women. Because Concha had more to say to one of these two women than to any of the rest, she turned a little in her direction. In the new arrangement, Concha seemed to be surrounded by her friends, and was able to shift her head and see three of them. She talked to the fourth, whose face, for Concha, was the least important, without turning.

Large articles of furniture in the center of the acting area tend to make good central action difficult. The placement of tables, sofas, or big chairs in this position is to be avoided whenever possible. But sometimes, especially

on small stages, the furniture just has to be in the middle
position, and the director is forced to work his human
design around it. How one director solved such a problem is depicted in Figure 14.

The play was Philip Parker's *Ancient Heritage.*[3] A
table, which served as a hub for the early action of the
scene, stood near the middle of the room. A crippled but
still dominating woman, Sarah, sat in an armchair a little

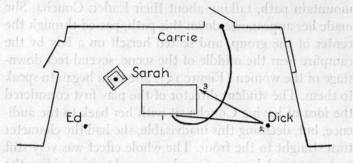

**FIGURE 14. MOVING BACK INTO THE SCENE TO HOLD CONTROL
OF IT**

From *Ancient Heritage.*

to the right and above the table, talking to her brother,
Edward, down right, and to a nephew, Dick, down left.
Carrie, the cripple's sister and the heroine of the play,
stood listening for a while in a doorway upstage, then
swept angrily down to the position marked 1, said a line
to Edward, and turned savagely on Sarah. Because Carrie
was on a line with Edward, she could speak to him and
still show the intense emotion written on her face.
Through the stormy scene that followed, Carrie addressed
each of the three persons present. The actress playing

this part was very uncomfortable in the position below the table. Two of the persons to whom she talked were on the sides of her, and one was behind her. Struggling against the table, she felt as if she were being pushed out of a firm hold on the scene.

Seeking a solution to the problem, the director discovered that the line of speech which Carrie was supposed to address to Edward alone could be divided. He therefore instructed Carrie to say the first part to Edward, then to walk over to Dick and say the second part to him, then to turn up to the position marked 3 and hurl her next words across the table to Sarah. Standing at this last position, Carrie was able to command the faces of the other three characters and to hold them attentive to her presence.

MANAGING THE CROSSES

The director has to consider not only the actors' positions, but also their movements, or "crosses," from position to position. In the best practice, the person crossing usually walks in such a way as to be visible from the beginning to the end of the movement, that is, in front of people and objects. In general, the active character is, at the moment, the most dramatic person in the scene. Consequently the director tends to confuse his design if he tucks the end of the actor's cross behind other objects or people.

Because movement across the stage is such an "attention-getter," the director sees to it that action of this sort is not made in front of a speaker—unless the speaker is of minor importance and is contributing merely vocal atmosphere. Usually, the director can manage the cross in such a way as to have it come just before or after the line of speech. If it is impossible for him to do this, he will have to split the speech at some logical point and rehearse the cross so that the actor moving will pass in front of the speaker at the moment of pause. This is usually not difficult to arrange because speeches during crosses are commonly pointed to those crosses. If splitting the speech seems inadvisable, the director may have to redesign a small part of the scene and place the speaker at some other point on the stage, where the cross will not interfere with the talking. (When the actor crossing is himself the speaker, he commonly moves during speech.)

The principle involved in these movements should be perfectly apparent. The audience wants to see the face of the speaker when he is speaking. It also wants to feel that the speaker can see the person crossing. The practice observed on some amateur stages of having the speaker, who is facing the front, talk over his back to someone moving behind him makes the spectators feel uncomfortable, to say the least.

In all his plans, the able director allows himself to be governed more by reason than by rule. Using his good sense, for instance, he would not insist on having every little movement on the part of servants, or other minor, atmospheric characters, pass downstage in front of the other actors; for that would not clarify action but clutter

it. And sometimes a downstage actor who is addressing a
moving figure has his face turned away from the audience. In a case like this, it would be only logical, of course,
to have the crosser pass upstage so that the speaker could
see him.

And what of a person in front of whom the cross is
executed? Frequently he finds that he is standing in the
path of the other actor's movement. The situation calls
for co-operation. The person before whom the actor
crosses "gives"—that is, eases himself back a little—to
help clear the path at the moment of the cross, while the
walking actor curves the path of his movement out a
few inches to aid the passage. After the second actor has
crossed the position of the first, the first steps quietly into
his original place. If he does this neatly, the audience will
not notice that he has moved.

ENTRANCES AND EXITS

People may be brought into a scene from any direction
—side, rear, or diagonal corner. When the stage is already occupied, the easiest, and therefore the most common, entrance, is from the side, since the figure coming
onto the stage from this direction can usually join the
group without dividing it. He simply adds his presence to
the design. An entrance from the rear, however, must
generally be anticipated by a shift of the people already
in the set. Some of the stage action in every scene tends
to hug the center of the stage, and this section must be

cleared so that the vision lines of the audience to the new
entrant may be unobstructed. This means that the figures
standing in the line of the entrance should move right
and left or, if they must stick together, in the same direction to one side.

If the entrance is meant to be a surprise, the figures in
the center will hold their positions until they hear the
telltale rustle in the hall or the voice in the doorway, then

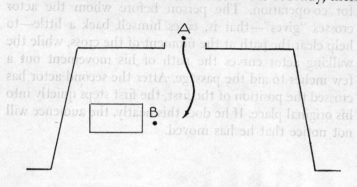

FIGURE 15. THE CURVED APPROACH

leap apart. If, however, the idea of suddenly revealing the
newcomer is not in the purpose of the director, he must
separate the people who are standing in the way before
the other character arrives. Movement, however, which
simply gives away the fact that the director is maneuvering for other movement, is bad. In order to make such
action appear to be perfectly natural, the director must
give careful thought to motivation. He may have to hunt
out the logical point (or points) for the clearing movements a number of speeches before the entrance.

Occasionally a figure is established, for dramatic rea-

sons, in a more or less fixed position near the path of a
rear entrance (under no circumstances would he stand
directly in it), and it may be inadvisable to move him.
In such a situation, the person entering can help to bring

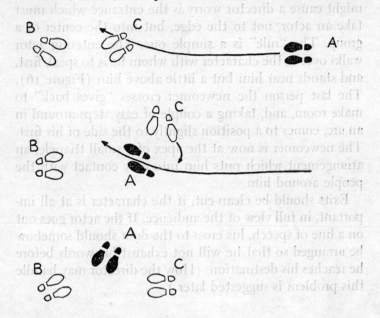

FIGURE 16. BRINGING A THIRD CHARACTER INTO A POSITION BE-
TWEEN TWO OTHER CHARACTERS

A moves in a curved line to a position a little above and to the left
of B, while C steps back, then moves down opposite B. (Action shown
in three phases.)

himself into view by coming downstage in a curved line
(Figure 15). It is to be assumed that the character entering would speak to, or at least look at, the figure already
present. The motivation for the newcomer's curved move-

ment would be his very natural desire to seek out the other man's face.

Most entrances from the side, as we have already stated, do not offer much of a problem. The only example which might cause a director worry is the entrance which must take an actor, not to the edge, but into the center of a group. The "rule" is a simple one. The entering actor walks over to the character with whom he is to speak first, and stands near him but a little above him (Figure 16). The last person the newcomer crosses "gives back" to make room, and, taking a couple of easy steps around in an arc, comes to a position slightly to the side of his first. The newcomer is now at the apex of a small triangle, an arrangement which puts him into easy contact with the people around him.

Exits should be clean-cut; if the character is at all important, in full view of the audience. If the actor goes out on a line of speech, his cross to the door should somehow be arranged so that he will not exhaust his words before he reaches his destination. (How the director may handle this problem is suggested later.)

TURNING

All turns on the stage should be executed with a minimum of waste motion. In other words, an actor who wishes to shift the direction of his face to speak to someone should make the shortest move around to him. If in doing this he can also keep his face in view of the audience, so much the better. But it is unreasonable for the actor ever to feel that he should move himself through two hundred and seventy degrees of a circle, just to display his face to the audience, when a quarter turn would take him straight to his goal. The vision line of the audience must always be respected, it is true, and, wherever the choice lies between two approximately equal turns, the actor should make that which will show his face to the spectator. But the dramatic contact lines on the stage come first, and the actor and the director should do everything in their power not to break them or entangle them.

"DRESSING THE STAGE"

One essential aspect of space design is what directors call "dressing the stage." This means, quite simply, keeping the stage in equilibrium, balancing the players more or less equally between the different parts of the acting area. Viewing the center of the stage as a central point of balance, the director distributes his figures on the two sides so that they will "weigh" properly against each other. The easiest method of doing this is, of course, to take the group present, divide it in two, and place half to the right and the other half to the left. But seldom is the director able to solve the problem so simply. In at least half of the scenes that come to his hand, the number of characters will be uneven, and he cannot put that odd man always in the center. Frequently, also, dramatic exigencies will force the director to distribute his people unevenly, putting two or three, perhaps, on the right (around an object of interest) and only one on the left. In situations of this sort, he can establish for the audience a sense of equilibrium by applying to his arrangement the principles of the teeterboard and shifting weights learned in physics. Figure 17 (*a* and *b*) illustrates how one actor placed some distance from the center, or fulcrum, point, may "balance" two actors placed near the center, and how two actors separated but on the same side may weigh equally

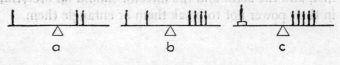

FIGURE 17. BALANCING THE STAGE

with four standing together a little from the center on the other side—and so on.

Equilibrium is affected not only by the number of characters, but also by their relative dramatic "weights." Certain characters count for more in point of interest than do others; consequently, their ponderable values in the design are greater. One Dr. Stockman standing alone at an end of a room in *An Enemy of the People* can balance easily all twenty members of a "compact majority" at the other end (Figure 17, *c*).

Still other elements which must be equilibrated are the architectural details of the setting and the property articles placed around them. The director would not mass a group of figures against the base of a heavy rock, right or left, leaving the other side bare of figures, unless he had on this empty side something of even more emphatic interest than the rock—such as a peculiarly vivid sky, or the wreck of an automobile. Some angle sets shape the acting areas within them in such a way as to provide more room for playing on one half of the stage than on the other. The balance point for scenes enacted here is shifted somewhat in the direction of the deeper portion of the set. The director should recognize this fact and try not to stuff too many figures into the shallow area (now on the longer arm of the teeterboard).

The element of lighting is the most important of the physical details. Brightly lighted areas are "strong," and dark areas are "weak." It takes several people in a weak area to balance one in a strong area, irrespective of the positions of these spots. One figure standing in a pool of light far over in one corner may hold the stage against ten in the shadows covering the rest of the stage. The tremendous effect of lighting on visual design cannot be overemphasized.

Up to this point we have considered the problem of "dressing the stage" as if it were only static. The most exciting part of stage design, however, is motion. Let the director do what he can to keep reasonably balanced the moment-by-moment aspects of the stage picture, especially during those quieter phases of a mass grouping, when the effect must "look like a painting"; but let him give his chief thought to those fourth-dimensional figures of design which can be completed only in time. Some of these figures may not reach satisfactory states of equilibrium before the passage of five minutes or more.

What, concretely, does this mean? Simply this: if a director places one dialogue scene on a couch to the right, he should not follow it with another dialogue scene in exactly the same spot unless he breaks the sequence with a little action on the left side of the stage; he should not keep two figures long around a fireplace in a left wall without moving one, or preferably both, over to the right for a change; if a man is seated right or left and a servant enters to speak with him, the director would not have the new figure come in on the same side, but let him enter from an opposite point so that the weight of interest would swing across. There should be compensation also for action in the center. One must not let an actor occupy this position for too long without making some movement elsewhere. Everything that has been said so far regarding the balancing of the stage from side to side applies with equal force, of course, to the balancing of the stage from front to rear.

TWO FUNDAMENTAL
"RULES" OF AUDITIVE DESIGN

If eyes are the point of departure for visual design in the theatre, ears are the point of departure for the auditive design. The lines of hearing must be clear both on the stage and in the audience.

Hearing differs from seeing in this respect: eyes are both active and receptive agents, whereas ears are only receptive. Auditive design, although it points to hearing, must take into account something else: the active voice of the player. Keeping this in mind, we can paraphrase the two leading "rules" for visual design and arrive at a pair of guiding principles for auditive design.

1. Keep the human presences on the stage in contact with each other through their mouths and ears.
2. Keep the voices on the stage, at all times, in easy hearing of the audience.

This means that the actors should speak always in such a way as to invite the attention and interest of the characters on the stage whom they are addressing, and the hearers should aim always to be responsive. The responsiveness indicated does not, of course, imply a continuous nodding or shaking of the head. It means simply a close listening and the stirring of something within the hearer which affects the outward expression of his face and posture. Larger movements of the head and body appear from time to time as a result of his primary reactivity.

Also, the voices of the speakers bear some relationship to the degree of the hearers' sensitivity. An actor should not shout to characters standing beside him; nor should he whisper to characters at a distance. The speaking and the hearing should all hang intimately together.

And every bit of the vocal activity on the stage should be fitted to the hearing of the audience. This seems a very obvious point, yet it is disregarded constantly by nonprofessionals and professionals alike. *The audience wants to hear what is going on between the actors on the stage.* This cannot be stressed too strongly. Because of the influence of the "natural" dialogue of the "talkies," perhaps, there has been a growing tendency for stage actors to speak "quietly"—so quietly, often, that no one out in front can understand them! On the other hand, some per-

formers insult their audiences by giving not too much silence, but too much noise. Spectators like to be shouted
at as little as being whispered to. It is all a matter of good
proportion.

COMPOSING
THE AUDITIVE DESIGN

The effective distribution of actors' voices around the
stage follows pretty naturally the lines of the visual design
already described. For that reason it does not seem necessary to take up separately here the adjoined problems of
vocal composition. If the director has in mind the two
basic sound rules set down in the preceding section, and
then arranges his actors so that visually they will form
contact with each other, point attention to the centers of
interest, and "dress" the stage, he should not have to
worry very much about the auditive plan.

It is true, however, that the director will have to give
some thought to synchronization. If the director does
not regard too seriously the following rules of thumb for
fitting speech to movement, he may find them useful.

1. Generally speaking, an actor should move on his
own line and remain still when another is speaking.

2. He should move on his own line when the movement demonstrates or emphasizes a point in his speech,
or when the line is important and a gesture will add to its
force, its "easiness," or its "naturalness."

3. He should not move on his partner's line, except when a pantomimic gesture on his part (such as a gesture of surprise or annoyance) is called for, or when a little movement (such as a quiet stitching of garments, shelling of peas, or whittling of a stick) will add to the naturalness or expressive quality of the whole scene, and the movement can be accomplished without distraction.

4. When a striking gesture must be used with an important line, it is often best to complete the gesture before speaking or, if the gesture must be used in the middle of the line, to hold the words for a moment in order to give place to the gesture. Because impressions are usually registered more quickly through the eye than through the ear, striking gestures have a tendency to obscure words.

5. An actor should never hold up the progress of the scene for unimportant movement. If he must make an exit at the close of a speech, and must walk across the room to reach the door, he is usually wise to break the speech somewhere near the end to make way for the cross (if the cross cannot be taken on a line), and to finish the speech from the door. This arrangement of the action prepares for a quick, clean exit of the speaker and the continuation of the scene on the stage without an unnecessary pause. There are, of course, situations in which this rule cannot be applied—when the speech is of such a nature that it cannot be broken reasonably, or when the manner of a walking exit is important in itself.

COMPOSING
THE ENVIRONMENTAL
SHAPES AND SOUNDS

The composition of the actors' movement and speech in a dramatic scene cannot be completed until the environmental factors have been disposed of. The contributing influences exerted by such surrounding forms as walls, doorways, costumes, and furniture are considerable. The importance of the part played by the setting is indicated clearly in the specific descriptions which introduce nearly every scene of a modern play. This description from the opening page of O'Neill's *The Hairy Ape* is typical:

> *. . . a cramped space in the bowels of a ship, imprisoned by white steel. The lines of bunks, the uprights supporting them, cross each other like the steel framework of a cage. The ceiling crushes down upon the men's heads. They cannot stand upright. This accentuates the natural stooping posture which shoveling coal and the resultant over-development of back and shoulder muscles have given them. The men themselves should resemble those pictures in which the appearance of Neanderthal Man is guessed at. . . .*[4]

How the scenic forms project the meaning of a play and intensify its effects, how they describe character, set the mood for action, and help the players tell the story, does not lie in the province of this chapter.* Here there

---

* Discussions of the dramatic function of scenery can be found in *The Stage is Set* (Simonson), *Stage Scenery and Lighting* (Selden and Sellman), and *Modern Theatre Practice* (Heffner, Selden, and Sellman).

is space simply to point out the general significance of the background forms, and to hint briefly how they may be integrated with the visual and auditory design of the players.

The environmental factors fall into two categories: visible shapes, and sounds. The visible shapes include scenery, stage "properties," costumes, and lighting. The environmental sound elements are not employed in every production. When they are present, they include incidental music and special sound "effects" (like bells, gunfire, wind, rain, the wash of the sea along a sandy beach). All these forms need as careful composition as do the central human factors.

The values derived from the proper contrasting of the players' faces and bodies with the scenery behind them has been indicated. The separation between the actor and his background is achieved first when due heed is given to the color of the walls. The painting of these surfaces in tones which approximate the complexion should be avoided whenever possible. Many dramatic scenes have been ruined simply by the fact that the faces of the actors failed to stand out clearly. When faces blend with their background, their expressions are lost, and the audience becomes quickly annoyed because it cannot read easily the movements of the players' eyes and lips.

A right relationship must be maintained also between scenery and costume, for the body of the actor is as important as his face. A green satin evening gown against green-tinted walls immediately makes negative the live figure which wears it. In like manner, a black suit worn

R	Right-stage
L	Left-stage
U	Up-stage
D	Down-stage
C	Center-stage
X	Cross
Ent	Enters
Ex	Exits
A., B., R.	Initials for characters—Ann, Bob, Richard, etc.
R. Ent UC X DR to A.	Example: Richard enters Up-center crosses Down Right to Ann.
▭	Table
C	Chair
●	Position of character
⟍	Path of movement (used instead of X in diagrams)
B. ▭ **A. R**	Example: Bob stands behind chair right of table, Ann sits left. Richard crosses below.
PHONE	Stage effect: phone ring
WIND	Stage effect: sound of wind
}	Music begins here
}	Ends here

MARGINAL SYMBOLS FOR THE PROMPT SCRIPT

in front of dark drapes tends to neutralize all the movements of the actor similarly shaded. The colors and texture of each costume unit must be worked out carefully with respect, not only to the background, but also to the other costume units in the scene. For the sensitive eye of the spectator there should always be a good balance between light and dark, between the larger areas of analogous hues for harmony, and of complements for accent, snap, and sparkle.

Furniture must receive the same kind of attention. The tonal values of the wood and upholstery should fit in with the general color scheme involving costumes and scenery. The shapes and placement also of the various objects must bear a plastic relationship both to the architectural features of the setting and to the figures of the players who sit in the chairs, lounge on the sofas, and stand by, or otherwise employ, the tables. Even little hand properties like cardboard boxes, weapons, or kitchen utensils have each a part to play in the composite design. Not infrequently a single small detail like a badly shaped, or badly placed, bowl will give a very distracting note to an otherwise well-planned scene.

Orderliness is always greatly to be desired. The careless placement of a large table or sofa right in front of a doorway through which important entrances are to be made is inexcusable. So is the huddling of furniture away to one side or up in the corner. The units should always be distributed in such a way as to make them serve best the needs of the players. At the same time, they should maintain a pleasingly balanced relationship to the doors, windows, and other shapes present. Sometimes, to keep the sight lines to the faces of seated actors unimpaired, sofas and chairs have to be placed at a 45-degree angle. But, in general, tables, sofas, and chairs should be placed in accordance with the rules of good "interior decoration"; that is, they should be arranged either parallel or at right angles to the rear or side walls of the set.

We come again to one of the most valuable media of design at the disposal of the composer-director, the lighting. There is no element which can be used so effectively for bringing out the plastic values of the actor's movements and keeping them distinct from the environmental forms. Lighting, flexibly used, serves powerfully to accent the faces of the principal actors, and to keep the attention of the audience focused on the strategically most important spheres of action. At the same time, it helps subtly to foreshadow. When the intensity of light is raised a little on a doorway or a table hitherto kept in the shadow, the spectator's anticipation is raised for important action he *feels* will shortly take place there. And while effective lighting is heightening and subordinating the various dramatic elements in the actors' movements, it is helping also to bring out those purely abstract linear, mass, and color relationships which intensify the spectator's enjoyment of the scene.

Walled rooms do not, of course, constitute all the locales for a play. Many scenes are placed on mountaintops, in the woods, on the prairies. For the setting, whatever it may be, the broad principles of order just described are applicable. The basic "rule" is simply that everything the spectator sees, animate and inanimate, must be in good composition.

And that rule applies also, obviously, to everything the spectator hears. Instrumental music, if it is used, must be planned in careful relationship to the actors' vocal design. So likewise must be planned the "effects" of wind and rain and even such apparently insignificant sounds as those of door buzzers and telephone bells. These, too, are elements in the larger tonal composition in which the players' voices simply take the leading role. The actors' performance, as we have repeatedly maintained, is essentially a dance and a song, and to the rounding out of that design all the environmental factors must contribute.

Chapter Eight

STILL AND MOVING PICTURES

THE PICTURE
ON THE STAGE

Viewed broadly, the central problem in visual stage design is the handling of dramatic imagery. The director-composer works, in every moment of a performance, with representative shapes—postures and movements which symbolize inward desire, all the forces which make each character a significant, driving unit in the play. Then the director shows, also by visible means, the complex relationships between the different shapes. The several individuals who make up a "scene" are placed opposite, beside, or around, each other, in such a way as to show clearly their mental and emotional attitudes toward each other. Naturally, people keep apart from those whom they suspect, dislike, disagree with; near to those whom they love, trust, agree with. The fundamental emotions ruling a situation are indicated by the *arrangement* of all the human factors involved in it.

Dramatic visual imagery seen in the large is the stage

"picture." Generally speaking, it has two functions. The first, and most important, is the one just intimated—the expressive. The picture shows visually the dynamic relationship between all the human units in the scene. The second function is a formal one. A skillfully designed stage picture affects the observer in the same way as a well-executed piece of sculpture, architecture, or painting, quite aside from the expressive values. On the stage sensuous line, radiant color, a fine balancing of mass and space, and sensitive toning play their part. The whole spectacle, even when it is viewed abstractly, is appealing to the eye. It has beauty.

Although we admit two functions for the stage picture, we must recognize that they are united, and that the ultimate purpose of both is the communication of dramatic feeling. A sensuously beautiful composition serves the purpose of expression much more efficiently than one which is ugly; for beauty puts the whole visual organization of the spectator into a receptive attitude. So we must finally include in our pictorial scheme, not only actors, but the clothes they wear, the scenery and properties around and in front of which they walk, and the lighting. All these factors are part of the expressive design.

Effective picturization in the theatre has two aspects: *still*—imagery considered in terms of the moment; *moving*—imagery considered in terms of a group of moments.

THE STILL PICTURE

When the director has given proper thought to the still-picture aspect of the stage design, the spectator sees, at each pivotal point of the play when action is at rest, a composition which is both pleasing and expressive. He notes that the picture says something about the emotional and mental attitude of every character in the scene considered individually, but especially as part of a group. And all the expressive values are heightened by a consideration of the formal values. Due attention has been given to both the selection and the arrangements of all the line, mass, space, and color factors in the expressive symbols, in accordance with certain basic principles. There are contrast, unity, and rhythmic vitality. Each player in the picture has been set off from, and, at the same time, fitted into, his background. He has been differentiated from other players (unless there is dramatic reason for sameness) in appearance, position, and pose; but he has also been united with them through common details of bearing, clothing, lines of sight, and other features. The opportunities afforded for rhythmical effects by the carefully proportioned repetitive spaces between the players, or between the players and the objects in the setting, by reflected facial expressions or directions for gesture, or by reiterated points of color, have not been overlooked. The ponderable details of form—people, furniture, architecture, areas of interest, and the like—have been so distributed on the two sides of the center that a sense of balance is established. All parts of the picture "hang together." The environment (scenery, properties, and lighting) has been harmonized with the human element in such a way as to produce that single impression which makes the moment of story here depicted understandable and enjoyable to the highest degree.

THE MANAGEMENT OF SPACE

The skill of a director as a designer is judged largely by his use of space. An experienced artist respects its value and employs it freely.

Space around a character enlarges his individuality. It gives him scope, makes him dramatically important. When personalities on the stage are crowded together, they may mean something as a group (as in a mob scene), but singly they lose power. Where character is set over against character, there must always be plenty of elbow room to allow the dramatic forces engendered between the figures to swing into action.

A separation of characters is especially necessary in scenes of strong conflict. The opposing figures, individuals or groups, should be placed well apart, commonly on two sides of the stage or on different levels. The greater amount of space there is between them, the greater will seem to be the break of accord. Objects such as tables and benches placed between them will increase

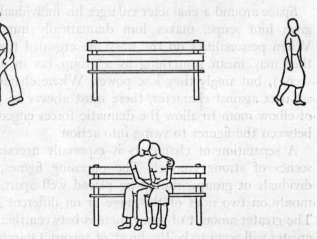

SPACE AROUND A CHARACTER GIVES HIM INDIVIDUALITY

Two lovers together appear to be one character. When they quarrel, they separate, become two different persons. The more space they put between them, the more "different" they seem to be. When they eliminate their points of difference, they become one again.

the sense of disunion.* When the battle is over, the opposing figures may "get together." Space is no longer valuable now because in the very act of agreement the characters have merged the most conspicuous parts of their personalities, those parts which stood out in conflict. Consider the boy and girl locked in each other's arms at the close of a lovers' quarrel.

Few directors in the nonprofessional theatre use space on the stage as effectively as they should. Amateur de-

DIFFERENCE IN CHARACTER MARKED BY A BARRIER
An object placed between two figures tends to emphasize the difference between them.

signers tend to huddle their actors, failing to open up the knots that constantly form, and to keep enough free air around each important personality. They fail to exploit to the full all the parts of a stage setting which might be used to give depth and variety to the action. This is especially true when the setting includes pocket

---

* In tight conflict, the symbolism offered by such barriers may have to take the place of space. Consider the common use of the table which stands between an angry husband and wife. Sometimes before the scene is over, however, the table will not be enough. The husband will turn savagely to the fireplace on one side of the room, perhaps, while his wife hurls her defiance from the doorway clear over on the other side.

areas behind sofas and tables or on secondary levels,
such as stairways and balconies. A good rule is to use
every part of the stage at least once before the scene is
over.

The spatial relationship in the stage composition constitutes such an important part of effective dramatic
imagery that too much emphasis cannot be placed on
this phase of design. The able director trains himself

STEPS AND RAISED LEVELS ENLARGE MOVEMENT IN SPACE
By adding height to width and depth, they give stage movement a
third dimension.

not only to think of space, but also to *feel* it, at every
point of his work. Although in the early periods of re-
hearsal he may sit on the stage, or close by it, in order
to make his help intimately available to the actors, he
soon moves his directing center well out into the auditorium, because only from this point can he adequately
establish a space perspective.

DOMINANCE
AND SUBORDINATION

Expressive composition requires a differentiation between the most important and the less important parts. That detail, or group of details, which most clearly sums up or focuses the meaning of the picture as a whole must naturally stand out. It must dominate. Its presence is made emphatic when other details are subordinated. This principle of dominance and subordination is a fundamental one for every kind of design. It is basic to the effect of painting, sculpture, and architecture, and the stage director should make himself familiar with the manifestations of it in these fields.

The emphatic detail in a dramatic composition may be a scenic form. In a certain moment of Philip Barry's *Hotel Universe*, the most powerful presence is supposed to be that of the horizonless sky. At other moments it is that point of the terrace which reaches mysteriously out into space; or the little fig tree with its almost human personality. The detail may be a property—an empty chair, an unopened box. Usually it is a man or a woman. Sometimes, when two or three act together with a single thought, it is a group. Whatever the object is, however, for the duration of the picture that detail dominates. Some of the devices for making a dramatic unit stand out have already been indicated. There may be at that point a heightening of color. Or the unit may be raised on a different level; or it may be surrounded by a larger

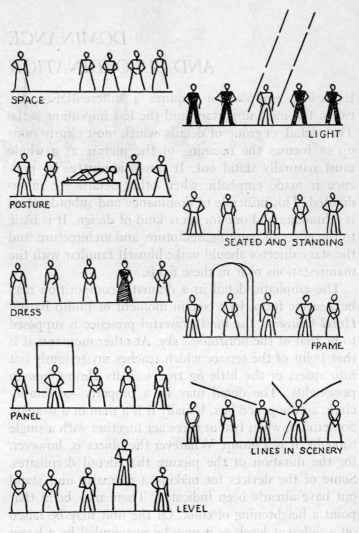

PICTORIAL METHODS FOR POINTING TO A PARTICULAR FIGURE

PICTORIAL COUNTERPOINT

Three simultaneous scenes of action united by the brooding spirit of a house and
the overhanging trees: Eugene O'Neill's *Desire Under the Elms*, produced at the
National Theatre, Stockholm.

STILL AND MOVING PICTURES

Scenes from Paul Green's *The Lost Colony*, produced on Roanoke Island, North Carolina, and Paul Green's *Johnny Johnson*, as presented by the Carolina Playmakers.

proportion of space than other objects. If the unit which must dominate is a human character, there are other devices available: difference in posture, difference in dress. He may be standing while others are seated, or seated while others are standing. He may be bareheaded when others are covered, and so on.

When a figure intended to be emphatic is made so by an arrangement of the scene as a whole, it is called

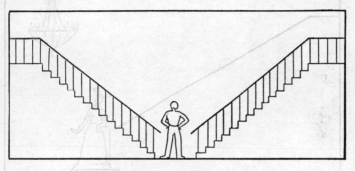

CONVERGING LINES POINT

the "center of interest." One of the most helpful factors in this kind of design is the eye lines of the other actors. Toward the point where all, or most, of the people gaze on the stage, there also will look the people in the audience. Skillfully arranged scenery also helps to point to centers of interest. Strong lines in the background, especially active diagonals leading inward, often direct attention to the points of particular interest. Because of the linear influence of a diagonal handrail, for example, the area around the base of a staircase is commonly a "strong" one. For nonrealistic plays diagonals are often

painted in, or the natural lines of a room, or other setting, are deliberately distorted for directional emphasis.
The most powerful spot at which an actor seeking attention can stand is at the converging point of several
bold lines. Another dominating spot is within a framing
line, like that made by a door, window, or archway, espe-

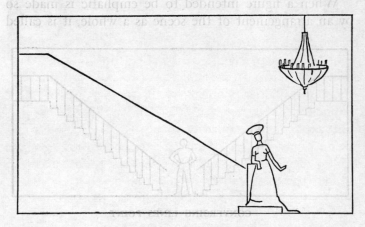

A STRONG DIAGONAL POINTS

cially when the section of the background also framed
is of a contrasting color and brightness.

The simple toning of a background wall helps greatly
to throw attention where it belongs. If the top of the
walls and the side corners are shaded subtly, the eye of
the spectator will naturally travel down the center toward
the lighter areas—where the emphatic characters usually
stand. The stage lighting is, as we have already observed,
a powerful assistant in the work of spotting these centers
of interest. As a matter of fact, it is more generally use-

ful for this spotting purpose than even the scenic forms, because it is flexible. While line directions, framing, and tone painting once executed have to remain set, the lighting can be changed. Hence, it is a potent factor in the building up of all pictures, able to pick out by greater brilliance or differential tinting the center of interest *wherever* it is placed.

Although much can be said regarding the influence of the environmental forms, the director can never lose sight of the fact that the human elements are finally the most important. If the lines of attention provided by the postures and eyes of the "supporting" figures are well planned, the audience will look to the right spot—despite misshapen scenery and misplaced lighting. Good scenery and lighting serve simply to reinforce the composition first made with human bodies. It is almost needless to add that every bit of the pointing described in these pages is futile if the figure serving as the dominating center is himself inexpressive. His own form must be the most eloquent object present, or the audience will miss in it that culmination of interest which it desires. If the figure of the actor is neutral, the whole composition is without meaning.

THE MOVING PICTURE

While we discuss the technique of building up the still picture, we remember that drama implies *movement*. Therefore, an effective management of stage imagery involves much more than the momentary three-dimensional appearance. In preparing truly expressive images the director (with the help of assistant artists) uses a fourth dimensional agent, time. The line, mass, color, and space qualities of the visual symbols are composed in motion-—blending, changing, contrasting, uniting, dividing, and joining again through a period equal to the length of the whole scene, from curtain rise to curtain fall. Many moment-by-moment still pictures are reformed in time to make one great mobile image.

Often the mobile design dispenses entirely with the still-picture factor, showing no moments in which, if the action were frozen, one would be able to see a perfectly balanced composition. In these passages the spectator feels through time for the various factors which together complete a period of the design. Each of the units extends, perhaps, over a minute, or even several minutes, depending on the nature of the action. Starting upstage, in a corner, or to one side, perhaps, the design will gradually unfold—bringing first one element, then another, then another into play—until every element present has contributed its part.

A simple example will show what we mean. In a dramatic episode concerning a great statesman some years ago there was a scene in which certain officials were disclosed grouped on one side of the stage waiting for audience. From a still-picture viewpoint the stage was clearly unbalanced. From a moving-picture viewpoint, however, it was excellent design, because it created anticipation for the element which would fill the void across the room. Soon a messenger entered to say that the statesman would shortly appear. The figure of the messenger was not clothed with enough dramatic interest to counterbalance the group of nervous individuals on the other side. He served practically, as he left the room, to increase the sense of want which was finally satisfied by the great form of the statesman himself. When his quiet figure entered, the attention of the audience went immediately to him. His side of the stage became much more weighty than the other, compensating finally in this way for the lack sensed in the period before the entrance.

Usually a play progresses through a combination of still and moving pictures. After a series of active moments the design comes to rest—or comparative rest—and then there is a still picture. Through the whole composite image (synthesized, of course, with a similar total auditory image) the spectator ultimately senses the meaning of the play.

THE DIRECTOR PAINTS THE STAGE WITH ACTORS

It should be repeated that, except in plays partaking of the nature of spectacle, there is today much less emphasis on the still-picture aspect of stage design than on the moving. In the productions of the last century and the beginning of the present there was a great amount of posing. Everyone who has seen a performance of that period will remember the "tableau." This type of obvious posing—holding the action, as it were, for the painter or photographer—is no longer considered good form. The still picture is used, but it is now made to be an integral part of the moving picture. Action flows into and out of the still pictures, and the postures and placement of the players at these moments are made to seem so natural that the whole pictorial arrangement appears to be more the consequence of accident than of design.

If we view the still picture as just one emphatic part of the larger moving picture, we can see the director's problem of stage design as a unity. As a picture-maker he is somewhat like a painter. The background—scenery and properties—has already been placed on the three-dimensional "canvas" of the stage. Now the director begins the most important part of his painting, putting in the human elements. He paints with actors. He strokes in a long line of dramatic color from the left, perhaps, then one from the right. These two lines approach, separate, cross, and circle around each other; and then other lines of color are brought in. The weaving design may at times include a dozen or more elements—if there is a crowd, many more than that. Up and down, in and out, from side to side, the lines go, making a marvelously live pattern of action.

If we view simply the movement of the feet on the floor, we see lines only. But the picture the director paints is not, of course, just a linear composition. Line movement becomes mass as soon as the actor shifts any part of his body away from its central axis. When he bends and twists his torso, raises or lowers his head, or lifts his arm, he is adding space to design. And, as we have pointed out several times, the actor's control of space can extend far beyond his bodily reach. By suggestive gesture (strengthened by eloquent vocal tones) he can touch regions of space far outside the limits of the stage.

So the director's "painting" is really a picture involving, besides lines of dramatic color, planes and masses of this color, which, if they are skillfully handled, fill the whole magic "canvas" of the stage. It is executed in three dimensions, plus a fourth, time; and it is all united with the composition of dramatic sound. Part of the stage picture may be still, part moving; but, whatever it is, it is affected by the basic principles of good pictorial design already mentioned. There are contrast, unity, and rhythm. There are balance, emphasis, and subordination, and an ever-present center of interest. And the picture at every moment fulfills its function of expressing something: it is *eloquent*.

THE COMPOSITION
OF THE CROWD SCENE

The director's problem with regard to the planning of the small-group scene is enlarged when he deals with masses of people. Crowds are naturally unwieldy, because by sheer bulk they tend to clog up the paths for free movement about the stage. The effective working-out of an "ensemble" scene invariably takes much careful planning. A poorly managed crowd becomes, not a credit, but a dramatic liability; it is either so inert that it affects the active factors like a shovelful of ashes cast on live coals, or it is so confused in its movements that it betrays all meaning of action.

On the other hand, a stage crowd skillfully handled is a powerful instrument for drama. It can image the forces of support or opposition in a way no single figure can. And by the magnitude of its approval or threat to a lone character it can bring out strongly the extent of that man's ambition and courage. Sometimes, as in certain contemporary Russian plays, or in the historical American plays of Paul Green (like *The Lost Colony*), the crowd is the protagonist. The "principal" characters serve simply to shape from the outside the attitude of the group or to give voice from within to countermotives between factions. The visual design of such plays is always complex. The picturization of dramatic scenes from another kind of play requires the use of two groups, in opposition. Those called for in the opening moments of *Romeo and Juliet* are an example. Productions of this play often cut the crowd fight to a desultory passage of arms between two or three men. Almost inevitably, then, the following scenes show some loss of force because the spectator has failed to see any adequately extensive image of the hatred separating Montagues from Capulets. Shakespeare brings out the fact that the hatred is so widespread that even the servants feel it, and fighting between the rival factions *fills* the streets of Verona. Three or four men clinking tin swords are poor symbols for this hatred. Conflicts between opposing masses, or between one mass and a man or a woman, are always tremendously exciting—when they are well managed.

The effective handling of a crowd scene demands from the director some courage, but mostly a clear head. First he has to decide just what kind of force the group sym-

THE CROWD MASSED AROUND ONE LEADER, DIVIDED BETWEEN
TWO LEADERS, DRAWN TO THE OPPOSING LEADER

bolizes, what is the crowd's essential character. At the same time he must determine what the group supports or opposes. The symbol for this second force will almost certainly be a single figure, or another group. The crowd's character and its disposition to support or oppose have to be worked out pictorially. If in the early stages of design the director will view the whole group as a single personality—standing together in one area—he will find that he can apply to its action most of the basic principles for pictorial composition already described for scenes without crowds. There must be the same arrangement for general balance, the same placement for sightliness, and the same movements forward, backward, and around. The difference will lie in the fact that, because

THE CROWD IS UNITED; THE CROWD SCATTERED CEASES TO BE A CROWD

the group is bulkier and generally less nimble than the single actor, its posturing and actions must of necessity be simplified.

But the crowd may not always carry a united personality. Moved by a common emotion one moment, it may be torn by dissension the next. This break-up of character must also be shown visually. The first sign of disunion is usually a swelling outward and then a scattering of the crowd. Elements which disagree with other elements seek to separate from them. If the spirit of conflict continues long enough, the crowd will part into groups, each rallying around its most lively representative. They will probably put as much space as possible between them.

One of the two groups may move over and stand by the very figure which a little while ago it opposed, showing now by its new position that it supports him.

If there is no clean cleavage of idea, and everyone in the group just disagrees with everyone else, then each in stressing his own personality will pull away from the others. In the act of scattering, the crowd ceases to exist. But perhaps, after the scene has progressed, all these different elements will begin again to feel a kindred sentiment about something—a person, an institution, a symbol of common well-being or advancement. Then they will get together once more and form a crowd.

SOME EXAMPLES
FROM THE LOST COLONY

Because the expressive values for large group scenes vary so greatly from situation to situation, detailed directions for composition cannot be very useful. However, some examples of crowd movement from a specific play may help to suggest what space factors are available for dynamic design.

The following several illustrations are taken from the author's production of Paul Green's historical play with music, *The Lost Colony*,[1] on Roanoke Island, North Carolina. The play is concerned with that little colony of men, women, and children which Sir Walter Raleigh sent to the American continent in 1587. The second act depicts the coming of the pioneers, the establishment of their settlement, their struggle, suffering, and final defeat. All the main action takes place on a large open-air stage representing a section of the log fort. There is an open chapel in the center, with two cabins on each side. The ground has two levels, the buildings being on the upper. Along the stockade at the rear runs a raised platform for the sentinels. Every foot of every part of the large stage (as well as two supplementary stages) is used at some time in the action.

The photograph facing page 257 represents a still-picture moment in the action of *The Lost Colony*. Seven women mending a communal fishnet stop their singing and gossiping to inquire from the midwife news of an expectant birth. She replies. Then action begins. The midwife goes stiffly out at the right. Now the old water-carrier, Tom Harris, with his Indian admirer, enters from the left, crosses to the group with the net, exchanges pleasantries, and goes out at the right. All his movements are large, loose-jointed, and crude, quite different from the dignified movement of the midwife. After another snatch of song, from away over on the left bank three little boys run in carrying fish, roots, and flowers. Their movements are small and quick. They stop for a moment to speak to one of the women, then run out at the right.

Certain effects have been created by having three kinds of movement cross the stage, and by varying not only the form but also the extent of the last. However, more crosses in the same direction (from left to right) would be tiresome. So, the next entrance, that of John

STRONG PICTORIAL DESIGN

The stage scenery, lighting, and action have united effectively to produce a dramatic picture marked by contrast, unity, and dynamic interest. The Group Theatre's production of *Gold Eagle Guy*, by Melvin Levy, setting by Donald Oenslager.

WEAK PICTORIAL DESIGN

The scenic elements are scattered, disunited; the lighting is flat; and the action lacks
any clear center of interest.

Borden, male leader of the colony, is from the right. His stride is long and manly. Because he starts in before the boys have cleared the stage, his large movements provide a moment of counterpoint for the little boys'. Another element of counterpoint is given in the simultaneous entrance of Manteo, the friendly Indian chief, from the opposite direction. In order not to counteract the main sweep of Borden's cross, he comes in only a little way. At the center group, Borden gives directions regarding the net; then, while the line of women carrying the net twinkles off to the right, Borden strides strongly over to Manteo at the left. Two artisans cross the stage from right to left to help compensate for the preceding predominantly left-to-right movement.

Suddenly, Old Tom runs in, also from the right, leaps to the upper level—not yet used in this scene—to ring the colony bell and assemble the settlers. They come in rapidly from all directions, not in solid masses, but loosely—for two reasons. Obviously, it would not be logical to believe that everyone would be at the same distance from the scene when the bell begins to toll. In the second place, the loose formation suggests a greater number of people and enlarges the effect of crowd action. Old Tom announces joyously the birth of Virginia Dare. While the colonists applaud, the minister and the child's father and grandfather hurry in from the right and make their way through the crowd to the chapel. Just in front of them, as they enter, comes a line of five small boys running just as fast as their little legs will carry them. They circle away around the whole body of the colonists and kneel by the corner of the chapel. This streak of the boys' bodies across the scene is designed to suggest, more clearly than anything else in the picture, the joyous excitement felt by the group as a whole.

Everyone kneels as the minister offers up his prayer of thanksgiving by the altar. In the middle of one of his sentences, however, there is a cry from a sentinel, away up on the rampart, that Indians are killing one of the colonists outside the stockade. There is a moment of frozen terror. Then a blunderbuss is fired. The men start out toward the right, the women shrink shrieking in a countermovement toward the left, and the lights black out.

In the next scene the baby is being baptized. Within the chapel stands the minister with the child, near the altar, and just below on both sides stand the godfather, the godmother, and three other principal figures. Outside, fanned out over a wide area of the lower level of the stage and the three steps leading to the upper, stand the rest of the colonists, facing up toward the chapel. After the brief baptismal ceremony, the minister hands the baby to its nurse. The group inside closes round the child for a moment while the greater circle below is still. Then the nurse steps out of the chapel, and the crowd surrounds her to look at the little form in her arms. While the surge inward is still in motion, Borden strides over to a loaded table at the left and calls the men to a drink of beer. As the men surge toward the table, the women sweep the nurse and baby down into the foreground near the center. A toast is drunk to the child, and before the merry sound of it is over, three musicians detach themselves from the group at the table, run in a wide circle around to the right corner of the chapel, and start playing. The nurse and child move to the center, where a ring is formed around them, and a country dance begins. The child is the focus for all the movements of the dancers. At the close there is a call for a speech from the governor. While he is taking his place on the upper level a little to the left of the chapel, and the main body of the colonists are moving over to stand around him, the nurse, accompanied by two women, is moving off toward the right.

So far, in this brief scene, the space in the chapel has been used expressively, as have also all the space on the lower level and most of the space on the upper level of the main stage. A few minutes later the raised platforms by the stockade come to life. Governor White is sailing for England. The mast of his ship moves past behind the scene. At the same time a number of colonists run up and along the platforms to wave their kerchiefs and call good-by.

In the two scenes described, the actions of the crowd for the most part suggest happiness. Other emotions are indicated in the last scene of the play. The long-expected relief ship from England has failed to arrive. It is a cold Christmas Eve, and the pitiful remnants of the colony, reduced by hostile Indians, starvation, and disease, are in desperate straits. Midway in the scene, Old Tom is decorating the chapel with holly while Eleanor Dare lights the candles on the altar. From away left comes the song of a procession bringing the Yule log. The half-frozen little line enters with tapers and circles round the campfire. After the main procession from the left has completed the first part of its slow circle, another little line of women and children from the opposite side moves around the fire, counter to the first. These are the people too weak to join the main procession. (Dramatic expressiveness and abstract contrapuntal design thus walk together.) The singing is punctuated by an occasional sob. Eleanor Dare ascends the steps toward the lighted candles. For a moment the hymn rises to a peak of feeling almost triumphant; then the men, women, and children kneel reverently in the snow, while Eleanor, standing erect, begins to pray.

One or two children whimper; a woman sobs, then another. Several voices cry to God for succor. A child's voice shrills out, and all at once the feelings of resentment, rebellion, and despair, long suppressed in the colonists, break out. While the great accompanying organ and chorus at the side of the stage support the sound of hysteria, men and women grovel in the snow, beat the steps, and crawl on their bellies toward Eleanor. One woman flings her arms high in the air and shrieks. Suddenly the form of a sentinel, benumbed by the cold, comes hurtling down from the raised rampart above into the center of the group. As he lies there groaning, the screaming crowd scatters to the right and left. Those away from the audience move on their feet, those near the audience on their hands and knees—partly to suggest that they are too terrified to lift themselves from the ground, and partly to preserve good sight lines from the audience to the prostrate form. One young man in terror runs a whole three quarters of a circle around to a position behind Eleanor. A woman near him moves toward him, and the two stand holding each other, shivering.

Borden strides in from the left and demands silence. He tries to lift the sentinel, who blindly attacks him before being led off at the rear. Someone cries for news, and, when Borden refuses to give it, the whole mutinous colony closes on him. At that moment the form of the dying minister slips out of the shadows and stands erect beside Borden. There is a gasp from the crowd. It falls back in wonder at the apparent miracle, then moves eagerly toward the minister. One young man falls to the ground beside him and clasps him passionately around the knees. Father Martin rests a hand on the young man's head, and the whole crowd becomes still. In a calm but authoritative voice, the minister speaks to the colonists and sends them to their cabins. Reassured, they move quietly away. And so the scene continues.

INDIVIDUAL FIGURES WHO POINT UP THE ACTION OF THE CROWD

All this space is given to the description of passages from *The Lost Colony*, not for the purpose of showing any special excellence in these particular designs,* but

---

* The basic plan for the pictures described lies, of course, in the playwright's own stage directions, and whatever credit the director deserves here depends on his success in visualizing and filling out the playwright's first intentions.

to suggest what *can* be done to make a crowd active. Far too often an audience is compelled to see just masses of people standing still. An inert crowd contributes nothing to dramatic imagery. There is no reason why it should be inert, because every crowd is obviously made of human characters, and each of them has the same kind of capacity for high feeling as anyone standing alone. In fact, the emotions in a group are commonly more intense than those outside. And feeling naturally expresses itself in action.

But it is true, as already observed, that it is hard to move masses of people flexibly. The general effects produced by their actions are of necessity broad. For this reason, the director who deals much with mass design soon learns the value of picking out certain details and making them say what the more bulky elements cannot. He points up the larger action in the special movement of one or two persons, placed where the audience is bound to see them. The line of little running boys emphasizes by specification the general group excitement in the first of the three scenes above. The movement of the musicians in the christening scene was inserted to create an anticipatory attitude for the dance. In the last passage there are three examples of this kind of designing: the woman who emphasizes the general hysteria by throwing her arms into the air and screaming; the frightened young man who by running in a circle points up the mass terror when the sentinel falls, and the woman who clings to him; and the second young man, who suggests the colonists' desperate desire for assurance by clasping the knees of the minister.

In the staging of the first act of *The Lost Colony* there are other examples of the same kind of design. The settings are in England. When a master of ceremonies at the garden party given in Queen Elizabeth's honor announces to the country people present that they too are invited to the feast, there is a general joyous response. Visually, this is made emphatic by the way two women on the edge of the crowd swing around each other. After the queen has entered and Sir Walter Raleigh has exchanged a few remarks with her, he introduces two Indian chiefs. Again there is general response, this time one of astonishment; but the feeling of the crowd is pointed up in the behavior of a small girl. At the first sight of the curious red men she runs back to tell an older companion about them. Then she moves forward stealthily to the front of the crowd and peeks shyly at the two savages from behind a man's legs. In the last scene of the act John Borden and the Spanish pilot, Simon Fernando, vigorously argue the merits of the colonial venture. The listening crowd is drawn into the verbal conflict, some on one side, some on the other. Most of the group responses are naturally broad. The playwright has sharpened up the sense of issues, however, by providing some individualized remarks, and the director has pointed up the visual aspect of the quarrel by seating two boys on the floor, prominently in the foreground. With their backs to the audience, they echo in pantomime, one for each side, the conflict taking place in the center.

MASS RISE AGAINST THE FORCE OF GRAVITY

BASIC MOTIVES

But, as important as are the individualized movements just described, they must not draw the attention of the director away from the fundamental movements of the mass as a whole. The basic motives for group action are, of course, the same as those for single. The composite organism, like the unit, is disposed to move toward objects which are beneficial, "attractive," and away from those which are injurious, "repugnant." It, too, tends to build up, lift up, objects which are dear, and to struggle with and destroy those things which it hates. The crowd,

MASS YIELDING TO THE FORCE OF GRAVITY

MASS MOVEMENT TOWARD A DESIRABLE OBJECT

like the individual, feels the tug of gravity and the forces of death—an end to activity—associated with gravity. Much of the most eloquent kind of mass movement is concerned with the push against this force, the reaching up toward heaven, toward life.

The crowd is affected also by those opposing impulses indicated in Chapter Three: (1) the impulse to move directly, violently, in order to satisfy primitive wants; (2) the impulse to curb these actions in order to preserve social order. A difference between crowd and individualized behavior lies in the proportional manifestation of these two impulses. The crowd is commonly much less influenced by the curbing impulse than by the primitive impulse to act directly. Everyone is familiar with the effect of mob spirit. A comparatively "civilized"

MASS MOVEMENT AWAY FROM AN UNDESIRABLE OBJECT

MASS BUILDING-UP OF A DESIRABLE OBJECT

man, who by himself would shrink from murder, may, in a crowd, lend his assistance to lynching. The next day, separated from his companions and alone once more with his social conscience, he will probably feel a strong pang of remorse.

A mass of people may be affected, of course, by many different kinds of motives, but those mentioned are, I believe, primary.

MASS DESTRUCTION OF AN UNDESIRABLE OBJECT

PICTURIZATION
AND DANCE DESIGN

Dramatic picture-making is, as we have suggested, a kind
of fourth-dimensional painting. The director, like the
easel artist, composes an eloquent visual design, using as
his basic elements line, mass, and color. The difference
lies in the fact that the artist's media are canvas and pig-
ments, and the director's are the stage and human bodies,
pointed up by costumes, scenery, and lighting.

While picturization in the theatre is seen as painting,
it must also be seen as choreography; for pictorial composition is fundamentally related to dance design. The
primary difference between the solo movements discussed
in Chapter Three and the group movements described
here is simply a numerical one. Effective mass action is
influenced by the same principles of rhythm, phrasing,
space control, and force control, as those which govern
the pantomime of the individual. Whether there is one
player or a hundred, good stage movement is essentially
a dance.

And the sounds uttered in the group scene must, of
course, be fitting to the action. If this mass movement is
dancelike, the mass speech must be songlike. For dramatic pantomime and dramatic speech, as we have repeatedly observed, are organically not two arts but one.

Chapter Nine

THE RESPONSE OF THE AUDIENCE

THE OUTER AND THE INNER MAN

An investigation of what the audience wants in the theatre occupies the opening section of this book. Since the spectator is finally the most important factor in the whole program of dramatic production, it is fitting that a consideration of his capacity for response should serve as a conclusion.

Let us look at the spectator as an individual. Practically speaking, he is made up of two parts: an outer man, an inner man. The outer man comprises all those features which are visually and aurally manifest to other people: surface appearance, outward action, voice sounds. We say of someone that he is five feet, eight inches tall; that he is thin, sandy-haired, light-complexioned; that his movements are quick and nervous; and that he has a baritone voice. That is the outward man.

The inner man, a much more complex being, can be roughly subdivided into two other parts: (1) the "mind";

(2) all those other inward activities concerned with biological well-being. The home of the mind is the cortex
and the subsidiary nervous system spread over the entire
body. The territory occupied by the second division includes the vital organs (heart, lungs, stomach, bowels),
the glands, and, to some extent, the striped muscular
tissue. The activity of most of this is automatic, involuntary. It is connected with the nutrition, preservation,
and reproduction of the individual. While one acknowledges the two parts of the inner man, one must recognize
the fact that they are so closely united that they can
properly be considered as one. All the vital functions depend upon the mind for co-ordination. The beating of
the heart, the opening and closing of the lungs, the
rhythmic contractions of the digestive tract, the secretions of the glands, are controlled by the far-flung net-
work of the mind.

If organic movement depends on the mind, the con-
verse is also true. The brain is a kind of control center
for man's mental activity; but thought is conditioned by
the whole nervous system and the organs of the body.
Glandular activity produces a profound effect on man's
thinking. It determines his "mood," and so the whole
drift of his reasoning. Says Alexis Carrel in *Man the Unknown:* "The dependence of mental activities and physiological functions does not agree with the classical conception that places the soul exclusively in the brain. In fact,
the entire body appears to be the substratum of mental
and spiritual energies. Thought is the offspring of the
endocrine glands as well as of the cerebral cortex. The
integrity of the organism is indispensable to the manifes-

tations of consciousness. Man thinks, invents, loves, suffers, admires, and prays with his brain and all his organs."

Then Carrel explains in more detail the interrelationship between mind and organs: "Each state of consciousness probably has a corresponding organic expression. Emotions, as is well known, determine the dilatation or the contraction of the small arteries, through the vasomotor nerves. They are, therefore, accompanied by changes in the circulation of the blood in tissues and organs. Pleasure causes the skin of the face to flush. Anger and fear turn it white. In certain individuals, bad news may bring about a spasm of the coronary arteries, anemia of the heart, and sudden death. The affective states act on all the glands by increasing or decreasing their circulation. They stimulate or stop the secretions, or modify their chemical constitution." [1]

Corresponding to some extent to the union of the two divisions of the inner man is that of the inner man and the outer man. Inward emotion tends to reflect itself in the expression of the face and the posture of the body. That thought processes are connected not only with the inward, but also with the outward activity of the body has proof in the commonly observed behavior of literary men in the throes of composition. They rise, sit, lie down, rise again, pace back and forth, light their pipes, go for a walk, return to their desks, all to stimulate the movement of their imaginations. Many writers are totally unable to create except on their feet.

Every external influence which affects the outer man invariably affects also the inner. The scent of flowers, the taste of food, the touch of a hand, all these make an impression on the mind, and all stir the automatic system into a response involving at least a minimum of emotion. Action of the outer body—walking, jumping, bending, reaching—also affects the behavior of the organs and glands, and so, in turn, the thoughts and emotions.

But while every exercise of the outside of a man motivates at least to some extent his inside, the reverse is not true *always*. In brain activity not involving creative imagination, the outer man may be quite still. Any kind of thinking, however, which involves a strong play of emotions is accompanied at all times by a strong *disposition* toward external activity. (Emotion has been defined as a stirred-up condition appropriate to overt movement.) In the primitive, uninhibited individual this agitation of the inner man is clearly manifest. But in the socially bred man, the outward action is often held in check. He may be seething inwardly, yet, when one observes his manner and listens to his voice, one can sense no reflection of the hidden movement. The man is "holding himself in." Many people hold themselves thus so constantly that the behavior becomes habitual.

AFFECTING THE INNER MAN IN THE SPECTATOR

From the viewpoint of the theatre, the outer man is, roughly speaking, the man of movement, whereas the inner man is the man of thought and feeling. Both the actor and the spectator are so divided. The basic substance to be communicated from the stage to the audience is thoughtful feeling. So the aim of the player, himself affected by a playwright, is somehow to extend his inner man out over the footlights and so affect the inner man of the spectator.

But inner man cannot touch inner man except through the medium of the outer. The actor must so order his external behavior that it will adequately reflect his inward

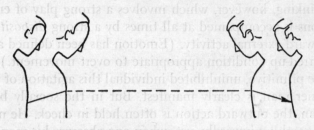

THE OUTER AND THE INNER MAN

The inner man of the player communicates with the inner man of
the spectator only through the media of the two outer men.

feelings and effectively stir the inside of the spectator through the exercise of a part, at least, of *his* outer man. Here, I think, is where so many earnest young actors go wrong. Wishing to be wholly honest in their work, to avoid the use of any external tricks, they hold tenaciously to the theory that if one *thinks* hard enough one is bound to project. Unfortunately, they fail to take into account the inhibiting influence of their own social habits. I have often seen these players concentrating so strenuously on a thought or an emotion that the scene has left them at its close completely exhausted. And yet the audience has re-

mained throughout quite unmoved! It has sensed none
of that inward activity—because the activity remained
inward.

Let us see now what biological apparatus the spectator
has for responding. He has the senses of sight and of
hearing. These are the most obvious. Other means, less
obvious but equally important, are the several other senses,
different kinds of muscular tissue, and the extensive nervous system which binds the many parts together.

What happens when a spectator observes an actor moving and speaking (not just thinking) on the stage? He
notes him with his eyes, and he listens to him with his
ears. Two senses are stimulated. There is good reason to
believe that they are not the only ones affected, but that
the whole sensuous make-up of the percipient is involved.
Evidence obtained in psychophysiological experiments
indicates that all the senses are interconnected. This
point is discussed at length in *Gestalt Psychology* by
George W. Hartmann.[2] We have, he points out, common adjectives, such as "bright," "brilliant," "loud,"
"pointed," for both visual and auditory sensations. As far
back as 1669, the distinguished anatomist, Thomasius
Bortholinus, noted that partially deaf individuals could
hear better in the light than in the dark, that even the
dim light of a candle improved hearing. In more recent
times, the eminent Viennese otologist, Urbantschitsch,
discovered that the hue of patches of color, so distant as
not to be recognized, was immediately perceived when
a tuning fork was sounded close to the ear. The tone of
the tuning fork even helped one to make out letters otherwise unreadable. Conversely, sounds which were on the

limits of audibility were heard clearly when lights of various colors were shown to the eye. Smell, taste, touch, sense of temperature, and other senses were all found to be modified by the presence of lights and sounds. Many musicians and others speak of "seeing colors" when they hear certain notes. One of the strongest proofs of the interrelation of the senses is a simple demonstration recently popularized by the Moscow biophysicist, Lazaroff. A piano key is struck, with the pedal depressed, and, while the tone holds the ear, an electric lamp is silently switched on and off. One hears, in the same rhythm, a swelling and fading of tonal intensity. When the eyes are covered, the intensity of tone remains unchanged.*

Thus it appears that the awakening of one human sense causes a stir (even if faint) in all of them. The more vivid is the sight, or the hearing, of the player's action on the stage, the more powerful tends to be the *general* feeling of that player's presence.

Sensation is the result of nervous impulses passing from outer sensitive areas to the inside. Sensation brings a mental reaction. At the same time it affects all the organic structure of the inner man. Also it *tends* to cause a responsive movement in other parts of the outward body not immediately involved in the local sensation. The

* Hartmann reports in the same book (p. 146) the evidence unearthed by another Russian scientist: "Using a telephone tied up with a low frequency cathode tube generator, Kravkov found that a tone of 2,100 vibrations per second increased the visual acuity of nine out of ten subjects tested with black figures on a white ground. This phenomenon was confirmed by the present writer for both high and low auxiliary sound stimuli, but even more astounding was the fact that simultaneous olfactory, tactual, and pain stimuli appeared to have equivalent effects in temporarily improving visual acuity."

mind, let it be remembered, extends throughout the whole nervous system, and there are nerve ends embedded in every muscle, even the smallest, from the crown of the head to the tip of the last toe. When the outward reaction is not controlled, it is manifest to the observer. A man touches a hot radiator, and he jumps away from it. He sees a missile hurled at him and he dodges. However, the same man, if he is a fond father, may without moving allow his baby daughter to pull his hair. He may listen to some very unpleasant piano-thumping by a neighbor and refrain from complaining. Nevertheless, the fundamental impulse to do something about it is there. The impulse is present, but it is checked.

Every sensory act, the psychologists tell us, is accompanied by feeling. It may be very slight, as when one hears a footfall or the closing of a door; or it may be intense, as when one receives a slap in the face. But, whatever the nature of the sensation, some feeling is present. And with the feeling there is always some motor activity. The movement in the muscular tissue may be worked out into manifest action, or, checked by a countcrimpulse, it may remain in an incipient state—just a tension. The movement may be general—both inward and outward— or it may be wholly, or almost wholly, inward, localized in certain tissues of the vital organs.* But, whether it is

---

* In a reaction associated with anger, for instance, the heart usually beats rapidly and the respiratory mechanism is accelerated, but the natural functions of the stomach are stopped almost completely. In other reactive states the reverse behavior may obtain. Certain glandular structures, such as the adrenals, are also affected. With the characteristic outer manifestations everyone is familiar: the blanched face, the "snapping" eyes, the clenched fist, the sudden movements of the legs and arms, the vocal explosion. Sometimes the outer activity is restrained, but with difficulty.

manifested outwardly or is hidden within the inner man, the stir of the muscles is there.

To put it simply, the sensing of any object results not only in mental activity, but also in a physical stir. Here lies the point we are trying to make regarding the spectator's responsiveness. Tracing the movements of the actor on the stage, he sees and hears him. But he does more than that; he feels the actor's mobile presence with his whole sensory apparatus. The total complex sensation which results is accompanied by a mental response in an active body. In the dramatic process, the actor's inner man is the generating agent, and the spectator's inner man is the object to be affected. The actor's outer man is the transmitting agent. Since inner and outer man are connected, and outer man *naturally* reflects the inner man when inhibitions are absent, the player's technique lies chiefly in the removal of the influence of restraining habits, and then in the selection, strengthening, and ordering of those movements and sounds which will most forcefully stir the sensory equipment in the spectator.

The spectator's outer man is then the receiving agent. That it plays also another part in the whole act of response will be seen presently.

PERCEPTION
AND PARTICIPATION

It has already been shown that the spectator comes to the theatre with a particular desire for the experience of action. As he sits waiting expectantly for the curtain to rise, he has his whole person set for an active response. When the moving bodies on the stage are revealed, the spectator's sensory-motor mechanism, already attuned, begins to work. He responds dynamically with every part of himself. His whole organism "moves" with the moving stimuli.

A sensory act, we say, leads to a change in the organism of the observer. But this change is not quite the same for everybody, nor for the same person under every condition. The change, both mental and physical, may be *more* one than the other. If it is primarily the first, it is intellectual; if it is the two together, it is organic. In other words, the observer may *perceive* action, or he may *participate* in action. He may listen to a rhythm given by a piano, recognize the meter with his mind, and remain otherwise (comparatively) unstirred. Or he may feel that rhythm in his own body and be moved to dance—or *feel* himself dancing, which is, practically speaking, the same thing. He may see a person walk across the stage and simply note the fact. Or he may also feel himself moving with the walker, taking the same steps. In a similar way, an observer may perceive one actor strike another actor, or he may also feel himself delivering or receiving the blow. He may note simply that a handsome young man is kissing a lovely young woman, and he may besides experience the approach of the girl's lips, sense the softness of her shoulder, and touch her hair.

Perception and participation are not, of course, opposites. They are simply two ends of a single reaction process. A response to stimuli begins as a perception. It may remain there, or it may go on to a point where the physical side of the organism is as deeply stirred as the mental. Then we have participation.

"FEELING INTO" OBJECTS OBSERVED

What constitutes the spectator's perceptive behavior should be clear to the reader. Just how he participates, however, needs to be explained.

Anyone who has attended a football game will remember how the people in the stadium seats play with the men on the field. If a favored player seizes the ball and starts down the field with it, his friends at the side lean a little in the direction in which he is going, putting out their own muscular and nervous energy to help him reach the distant goal line. They "feel into" his action. Similar behavior may often be noted at a horse or dog race, or at a track meet. Sometimes the spectator "runs" so hard with his favorite entrant that his body aches and there is no breath left in him.

The impulse to feel out physically the qualities of objects that interest us is natural to all. The objects need not be in motion or even animate. We see a polished granite ball, and we sense its smoothness, roundness, and weight, at a distance. While we contemplate its heaviness, to us comes no urge to dance, or to walk lightly on our toes. We "feel" solid, established, just as if we were

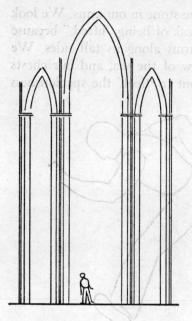

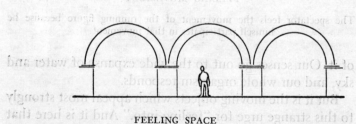

FEELING SPACE

One not only *perceives*, but also *feels*, the difference between the low round arch and the high pointed arch. The Roman type of arch feels constrained, bound to solid earth. The Gothic type, unconfined, reaches away from earth. The sense of height in the tall arch is intensified when the man standing within it imagines himself running his hands up along the sides of the lofty piers.

holding the great bulk of the stone in our arms. We look
at a marble column and speak of being "lifted," because
inceptively we reach our arms along its tall sides. We
come suddenly upon a view of the sea, and our chests
rise and our palms reach out to "feel" the spaciousness

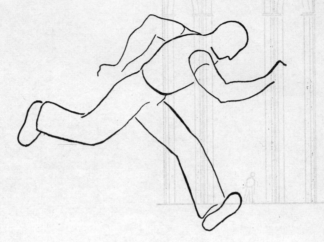

FEELING MOVEMENT

The spectator feels the movement of the running figure because he
himself participates in that movement.

of it. Our senses go out to the wide expanse of water and
sky, and our whole organism responds.

But it is the moving objects which appeal most strongly
to this strange urge for "feeling into." And it is here that
we discover the truer meaning of participation. We see a
sailboat, and our senses are projected to it. But we not
only feel the boat pass us; we sense within ourselves

THE FEELING VALUE OF SCENIC SHAPES

As soon as the curtain rises, and before any movement takes place, the spectator feels the dramatic spiral approach to the altar and the exciting lift of the columns. Model by Norman Bel Geddes for Gluck's opera *Iphigenia in Aulis.*

Thomas Bouchard

THE FEELING VALUE OF RHYTHMIC ACTION

A strong appeal to sensuous response is here produced by a dance movement: the Charles Weidman Group in *New Dance*.

something of its graceful motion. When we watch a swinging pendulum for a long time, we tend to sway with it ourselves. Who has not felt himself on occasion rising and falling while watching the movement of a pile driver, or twisting and bending with a blown tree? When such objects become human, and are clothed with "significant" emotional symbols, their appeal to our participatory responsiveness is even stronger. A man in a restaurant in a university town told the author that, watching closely the behavior and expressions of the boys coming in to supper from an afternoon at a motion picture, he could tell the type of film they had seen—gangster, romantic, comic. Lee Mitchell describes a moment in his production of *Œdipus* at Northwestern University, when the messenger came onto the stage to describe the horrible death of Jocasta. When she lifted her hands to her face to shut out the image of what she had seen, many in the audience lifted their hands also. A woman at the showing of the film *Hurricane* was observed to sway with a swaying tree in the picture. A dancer tells of a studio recital in which one series of movements made him breathe heavily. He discovered that one of the spectators was breathing quite audibly in time with him. The tendency to imitate action in which we are interested is common to us all, though the movement usually remains in an incipient state only.

The spectator's reaction here described constitutes simply, let us repeat, a full, organic response—one which includes not only an eye-and-brain recognition of an object, but also an excitation of all the senses and a stir of muscles somehow related to the action seen. The stimu-

lating action may be actual, or it may be implicit, like the
crouch of a cat which sets our inward muscles tingling
just before it leaps on the mouse.

The moving "objects" sensed in music provide one of
the strongest appeals for the feeling-into response. One
feels himself "singing" with a singer, humming or beating
time with an orchestra. In an even more intensive way,
one is carried along by the moving elements of the tone
structure. Harmony, closely followed, gives one the sense
of excursion and return. Tempo and rhythm suggest hur-
ried or deliberate movement, facile or obstructed progress, agitation or languor.[3]

The appeal to the human impulse to feel actively into
objects is used constantly in pictorial composition. The
drawings which serve to illustrate principles of action in
Chapter Five suggest how even simple lines may have this
stimulating quality. The pictures facing pages 137 and
187 present other examples. Many works of architecture
and sculpture possess the same kind of participatory appeal. Pointing out our tendency to transcribe ourselves
into a design that embodies structure, Joseph Hudnut,
Dean of the School of Design of Harvard University, says:
"We translate the organism of our own bodies into the
ossature of arches and columns, into their strain and effort, their pressures and resistances, and we are therefore
the more conscious of the harmonies that they embody.
The same process makes us more vividly aware of those
formal relationships that are realized in representations
of the human body [sculpture] than in pure forms devoid
of all humanity. The effort, or repose, of muscles, the interaction of the framed skeleton, the equilibrium that ap-

pears to be constantly sustained, provoke a feeling of life in the stone before us; we enter into it and share whatever formal beauty it has attained." [4]

Japanese paintings have long been famous for both the "grace" and "vigor" of their line. That their effect depends in large part on what the spectator finds when he "feels into" them, and that the Japanese artist recognizes this fact, is indicated in the following quotations from Henry P. Bowie's *On The Laws of Japanese Painting.*

"A distinguishing feature in Japanese painting is the strength of the brush stroke, technically called *fude no chikara* or *fude no ikioi.* When representing an object suggesting strength, such, for instance, as a rocky cliff, the beak or talons of a bird, the tiger's claws, or the limbs and branches of a tree, the moment the brush is applied the sentiment of strength must be invoked and felt throughout the artist's system and imparted through his arm and hand to the brush, and so transmitted into the object painted; and this nervous current must be continuous and of equal intensity while the work proceeds. If the tree's limbs or branches in a painting by a Kano artist be examined, it will astonish anyone to perceive the vital force that has been infused into them. Even the smallest twigs appear filled with the power of growth. . . .

"One of the most important principles in the art of Japanese painting—indeed, a fundamental and entirely distinctive characteristic—is that called living movement, SEI DO, or *kokoro mochi,* it being, so to say, the transfusion into the work of the felt nature of the thing to be painted by the artist. Whatever the subject to be translated

—whether river or tree, rock or mountain, bird or flower, fish or animal—the artist at the moment of painting it must feel its very nature, which, by the magic of his art, he transfers into his work to remain forever, affecting all who

JAPANESE BRUSH WORK

Figures in Japanese brush drawings *feel* active because the spectator senses through the dynamic brush strokes the movement of the man or animal which the artist himself felt when he applied the ink to the paper. (From *Brushwork Study* by Seiho. Courtesy of The Robert-Lee Gallery, Inc., New York.)

see it with the same sensations he experienced when exe-
cuting it. . . .

"The Japanese artist is taught that even to the placing
of a dot in the eyeball of a tiger he must first feel the
savage, cruel, feline character of the beast, and only under
such influence should he apply the brush. If he paint a
storm, he must at the moment realize passing over him
the very tornado which tears up trees from their roots
and houses from their foundations. Should he depict the
seacoast with its cliffs and moving waters, at the moment
of putting the wave-bound rocks into the picture he must
feel that they are being placed there to resist the fiercest
movement of the ocean, while to the waves in turn he
must give an irresistible power to carry all before them;
thus . . . reality is imparted to the inanimate object."

Mr. Bowie further illustrates the purpose of the Japanese artist with the story of the Chinese master, Chinanpin: "It is related of Chinanpin, the great Chinese painter,
that an art student having applied to him for instruction,
he painted an orchid plant and told the student to copy
it. The student did so to his own satisfaction, but the
master told him he was far away from what was most
essential. Again and again, during several months, the
orchid was reproduced, each time an improvement on
the previous effort, but never meeting with the master's
approval. Finally Chinanpin explained as follows: The
long, blade-like leaves of the orchid may droop toward the
earth but they all long to point to the sky, and this tendency is called cloud-longing (BO UN) in art. When,
therefore, the tip of the long slender leaf is reached by the

brush the artist must feel that the same is longing to point to the clouds. Thus painted, the true spirit and living force (*kokoromochi*) of the plant are preserved." [5]

The moving force felt to be in the leaf by the artist who contemplated it is placed by him in the brush strokes of his painting; and this same force is re-experienced by the spectator who looks at and "feels into" the picture. By Chinanpin's—and all other great artists'—standards, a painting is fully successful only when it commands not just perception, but also participation. The spectator recognizes, and besides he *feels*, because his whole organism has been fully aroused in response.

THE INFLUENCE OF PAST EXPERIENCES ON THE RESPONSE

But the degree to which a man's complete self will be awakened by the sight of a painting depends on a number of factors outside the immediate control of the artist. The principal of these factors is the spectator's previous experience. One can imagine, for instance, that a young city-bred child, who has never seen growing flowers, views Chinanpin's orchid. The longing of the leaves to point upward would doubtless remain unfelt by the child, and the dynamic "vigor" of the brush strokes would therefore be passed unnoticed. A person, however, who has watched the lives of growing plants, and has felt in their struggles something akin to his own desire to conquer

ACTIVE DRAWINGS

The person who glances at these drawings senses through their crisply moving lines the action felt by the artist when she made them. Impressions of the Weire Brothers, precision dancers of the *Straw Hat Revue*, by Polly Perkins. (Reproduced by courtesy of *Theatre Arts Monthly*.)

gravity and reach to the sun, would respond to the painting immediately.

It is extremely interesting to observe artists examining and discussing other artists' canvases. Almost invariably they supplement their verbal comments with sensuous gestures of their hands. They are feeling through the drawing and the brush strokes of the artist whose work they are viewing. Their application is naturally conditioned by their own past experience in painting. Musicians likewise often demonstrate the values of their training when they read a composer's score with a movement of their fingers. Three instrumentalists were recently heard to comment on a recital given by a famous trio. All spoke enthusiastically about the rendering as a whole, but one liked particularly the technical performance of the pianist, whereas the other two favored respectively the violinist and the 'cellist. Then it was revealed that the three commenting musicians themselves played the three different instruments! The previous experience of each conditioned his special appreciation for one element of the performance.

Dancers give similar testimony. Frequently even a little exercise on the studio floor will change completely a young student's responsiveness to a trained performer's work. A dance passage which left her unmoved when seen two weeks before now makes her "feel like jumping out onto the stage floor and doing the same steps!" Such skilled men as machinists, craftsmen, and doctors say the same thing with regard to the influence of past experience. A surgeon watching another operate tells afterward how he "made every move with" the doctor performing.

However, the appreciation of fine objects and actions does not necessarily depend on previous experience directly associated with that particular thing. One does not have to have crossed an ocean to feel something of its expanse. One does not have to have flown in an airplane to feel something of its speed. In a hundred ways in the everyday life of the average person there are little experiences of moving, climbing, descending, reaching, retreating, exerting one's effort, perfecting one's skill, which serve as a basis for our sensuous and dynamic understanding of new objects and actions. These past experiences are retained in the human organism as a sort of vast reference bureau. There they give meaning and direction to each succeeding response.

Artists in every field have to consider carefully how and to what extent habits of living have shaped the sensitivity of their spectators and auditors and adapt their techniques accordingly. This is especially true in the theatre, where the sensatory appeal must be direct and immediate. Both the subject matter and the style in which it is developed and projected have to be related to the audience's experience. If they are not so related, the audience fails to feel into the action, and the interest lags.

THOUGHT
IN THE RESPONSE

Both the perceptive and the participatory elements of response are fundamentally sensuous. They do not, of

course, constitute the whole of the observer's reaction to
a moving object. The act of perceiving, running through
to participation, is the prelude to intellectualization.
What a man feels sensuously about an observed action
leads to thought about it. The form of that thought is
very important to the artist who designs the action; for
upon what the spectator thinks after he has felt a sensation depends the ultimate success of the design.

But, and this is the message of this chapter, there cannot be rich thought without adequate sensation. If the
artist wishes the observer of his work to think deeply
about it, he must first provide the observer with stimuli
which will effect a whole-organism response. I feel very
strongly that critics in every field of the dynamic arts (music, dance, and drama) have failed to give proper value
to the sensuous foundations. With John Martin, the
dance critic of the New York *Times*, I agree when he says
in *America Dancing:* "Education has made a fetish of
intellectualism and has placed no value on the resources
of the body. But the intellect as an independent agency
is without value. Unless it is given material to work with,
it is powerless, for it can of itself establish no contacts
with the outside world. It is dependent upon the sensory
and motor equipment to put before it the problems of
the individual in his relation to his environment. Otherwise, it must deal with abstraction or with the rehashing
of past testimony." [6]

THE RESPONSE
IN THE THEATRE

In the light of what has been said in the last few pages,
let us go back to the spectator in the theatre and, by
means of an example, sum up the steps in his response.
He sees before him on the stage three persons, two men
and a woman, dressed in costumes of the late nineteenth
century. One man is tall, well-built, middle-aged; the
other, slight and boyish. The woman, in her early thirties,
is of medium height, with brown hair, and her name is
Candida. The larger man, her husband, is the Reverend
Morell, and the boyish man, a poet, is Eugene Marchbanks. They are discussing which of the two men Candida
will choose. Marchbanks, on one side, is declaring that he
possesses the qualities Candida must love. Morell, on the
other side, utters just one word and is silent. He strides
back and forth, then sits down suddenly at the fire with
his head in his hands. Candida, between, looks with a
little humorous smile from one to the other. Then her
face becomes serious.

The spectator has noted several details of appearance
and action. His response so far has been basically perceptive. It may remain so. If it does, he will retain in
his memory some visual and auditory facts, but he will
be comparatively unstirred by them. On the other hand,
the response may go further. Instead of merely watching the figures moving on the stage, the spectator may
feel into them. Sensing in his own body the youthful

eagerness of the poet's posture, feeling as if he himself were uttering the passionate words, the spectator comes to the same emotion as that which motivates the young man's actions. Feeling in turn the clergyman's stride across the room, the sudden slump of his body in the chair, and the desperate movement of his hands, he touches the emotion which possesses Morell, with almost no word spoken. And the spectator senses out Candida's smile, the change of that expression, the momentary stillness of her body; then the tone of her voice as she utters her decision. So the observer arrives at an understanding of that decision, not with the brain alone, but with his body also. The man "out front" has participated sensuously in the action depicted on the stage. That act of participation forms the foundation for his intellectual appreciation.

It has been assumed that the actors on the stage have provided in their action suitable stimuli for the spectator's response. But perhaps another company presents the same scene, and, although they speak the words clearly, exactly as written, they inflect monotonously and move about woodenly. The young poet may shift his feet needlessly; the clergyman may pace with steps too long or short, and sit clumsily; and Candida's smile may be too broad, or fail to appear at all. The spectator now has the same words and the same basic gestures for his ears and eyes; but he will remain unstirred, because he no longer has an impulse to feel into actions so contrary to his own expressive urges. He may fall asleep from boredom, or he may become annoyed and leave the theatre. The spectator has not been aroused sensuously—at least, in the right way —and so the play has failed.

CONCLUSION

It may be objected that the picture of the spectator's response has been oversimplified in this chapter. The simplification will have to be admitted. But it has been done with deliberate purpose, to emphasize the importance of that phase of dramatic experience which is so often slighted in discussions of the theatre, the fully sensuous response. The term *sensuous* has, for some reason, acquired an unpleasant connotation in art criticism, and it has frequently therefore been dropped from the vocabularies of the more serious writers, actors, and directors. This is a mistake, I think, for an appeal to the senses is, and should always be, recognized as the starting point of technique. It is only when the senses are badly used that "sensuousness" is to be avoided.

The complete picture of the spectator's response to action on the stage involves, of course, several important factors not touched on in this chapter. And the term "participation" must be recognized as representing a phase of response which the spectator cannot experience to an equal degree in every part of a well-designed play. In scenes where the stage characters' minds are in an objective frame—when facts are being stated, or purely intellectual points are being discussed, for instance—it is not to be expected that the spectator will "feel" largely into the characters' bodies. And in comedy scenes the spectator may hold his sensuous feelings pretty consistently aloof, commenting on the action mostly with his mind. The more extreme the comical behavior seen, the more objective the observer tends to become.

But it is my belief that the sensuous, subjective element is never wholly absent, even when the characters, as characters, are doing nothing in which the spectator would wish to participate. At such moments the spectator continues to "act" with the player. He finds a pleasure in following sensuously a skillful actor's delivery of his lines and pantomime; for, through this, he feels in himself the same freedom, rhythm, effectiveness of movement.

To sum up: it is my conviction that no dramatic artist can hope successfully to project character and story until he has given attention to sensuous appeal. This appeal must be not to two senses and a corner of the brain only, but to the whole of the spectator's organism.

And the performance which most forcefully presents this appeal is one composed of fundamentally *natural* action, touched by the magic of dance and song.

REFERENCES

CHAPTER I

1. Daniel Gregory Mason, *From Song to Symphony* (Oliver Ditson Company, Boston, 1924), pp. 91–92.
2. Havelock Ellis, *The Dance of Life* (Houghton Mifflin Company, Boston, 1923), pp. 59–60.
3. F. Max Müller, *Auld Lang Syne* (Charles Scribner's Sons, New York, 1898), p. 42.
4. Alastair St. Clair Mackenzie, *The Evolution of Literature* (Thomas Y. Crowell Company, New York, 1911), pp. 134, 136, 146–147.
5. Havelock Ellis, *op. cit.*, pp. 42, 43–45. William Ridgeway, *The Dramas and Dramatic Dances of Non-European Races* (Cambridge University Press, Cambridge, England, 1915), pp. 8–10.

CHAPTER II

1. A. E. Crawley, "Processions and Dances," *Encyclopaedia of Religion and Ethics*, edited by James Hastings (Charles Scribner's Sons, New York, 1922), p. 359.
2. Curt Sachs, *World History of the Dance* (W. W. Norton & Company, New York, 1937), p. 5.
3. Curt Sachs, *op. cit.*, p. 49.
4. John Lawson, *History of North Carolina* (The Observer Printing House, Charlotte, North Carolina, 1903), p. 103.
5. Curt Sachs, *op. cit.*, p. 53.

6. Yrjö Hirn, *The Origins of Art* (The Macmillan Company, New York, 1900), pp. 89–90.

7. James L. Mursell, *The Psychology of Music* (W. W. Norton & Company, New York, 1937), pp. 27–30. Harry Porter Weld, "Psychology of Musical Enjoyment," *American Journal of Psychology*, Vol. XXIII, p. 298.

8. John Lawson, *op. cit.*, p. 103.

9. Charles M. Diserens, *The Influence of Music on Behavior* (Princeton University Press, Princeton, 1926), pp. 108, 115, 117, 121.

10. Walter Bradford Cannon, *Bodily Changes in Pain, Hunger, Fear and Rage* (D. Appleton–Century Company, New York, 1929), p. 228.

11. Charles M. Diserens, *op. cit.*, pp. 27–32.

12. Lafcadio Hearn, *Karma* (Boni and Liveright, New York, 1918), pp. 70–109.

13. Charles M. Diserens, *op. cit.*, p. 62. Alastair St. Clair Mackenzie, *The Evolution of Literature* (Thomas Y. Crowell Company, New York, 1911), pp. 98–100, 148–150.

14. Isaac Goldberg, *Tin Pan Alley* (The John Day Company, New York, 1930), p. 292.

15. Charles M. Diserens, *op. cit.*, pp. 45, 46, 48.

16. Curt Sachs, *op. cit.*, p. 49.

17. James L. Mursell, *op. cit.*, pp. 21–30.

18. Ellsworth Jaeger, "Nature's 'Jitterbugs,'" *Nature Magazine*, Vol. 33, No. 7 (August–September, 1940), pp. 395–397. Curt Sachs, *op. cit.*, p. 9. Richard Wallaschek, *Primitive Music* (Longmans, Green & Co., London, 1893), p. 242.

19. Jack McLaren, *My Crowded Solitude* (T. Fisher Unwin, Ltd., London, 1926), pp. 54–55.

20. Wolfgang Köhler, *The Mentality of Apes*, translated by Ella Winter (Harcourt, Brace and Company, New York, 1925), pp. 318, 326–328.

CHAPTER III

1. Carl Emil Seashore, *The Psychology of Musical Talent* (Silver Burdett Company, New York, copyright 1919), p. 115 (see also Chapter V). Quoted by permission of the publishers.

2. Jerome Beatty, "An American Helps Italy Over the Hurdles," *American Magazine*, November, 1938.

3. Paul Green, *The House of Connelly*. Copyright 1931 by Paul Green, all rights reserved. Reprinted by permission of the author and Samuel French, New York.

4. Jesse F. Williams, *Principles of Physical Education*, revised edition (W. B. Saunders Company, Philadelphia, 1932), p. 80.

CHAPTER IV

1. James L. Mursell, *The Psychology of Music* (W. W. Norton & Company, New York, 1937), p. 19.

2. John Dewey, *Art as Experience* (G. P. Putnam's Sons, New York, 1934), p. 237.

3. Mabel Elsworth Todd, *The Thinking Body* (Paul B. Hoeber, New York, 1937), p. 217.

4. James L. Mursell, *op. cit.*, p. 26.

5. Paul Eldridge, *Vanitas* (The Stratford Company, Boston, 1920).

6. Emlyn Williams, *A Murder Has Been Arranged*. Copy-

right 1931 by Emlyn Williams, all rights reserved. Reprinted by permission of Samuel French, New York.

7. Douglas Moore, *Listening to Music* (W. W. Norton & Company, New York, 1932), p. 40.

8. James L. Mursell, *op. cit.*, pp. 35–36.

9. Alastair St. Clair Mackenzie, *The Evolution of Literature* (Thomas Y. Crowell Company, New York, 1911), p. 150.

10. Arthur Schopenhauer, *The Philosophy of Schopenhauer*, edited by Irwin Edman (The Modern Library, Random House, New York, 1928).

11. John Dewey, *op. cit.*, p. 236.

12. Richard Wallaschek, *Primitive Music* (Longmans, Green & Co., London, 1893), pp. 75–76.

13. John Steinbeck, *Of Mice and Men*, p. 29. Copyright 1937 by John Steinbeck. By permission of The Viking Press, Inc., New York.

14. John Steinbeck, *Of Mice and Men*, pp. 170–172. Copyright 1937 by John Steinbeck. By permission of The Viking Press, Inc., New York.

15. Albert R. Chandler, *Beauty and Human Nature* (D. Appleton–Century Company, New York, 1934), p. 194.

CHAPTER V

1. John Dewey, *Art as Experience* (G. P. Putnam's Sons, New York, 1934), p. 14.

CHAPTER VI

1. Milton M. Smith, *Book of Play Production* (D. Appleton–Century Company, New York, 1926), p. 2.

2. Douglas Moore, *Listening to Music* (W. W. Norton & Company, New York, 1932), p. 69.

3. Maxwell Anderson, *Valley Forge* (Anderson House, Washington, D. C., 1934), p. 22.

4. Erma Green and Paul Green, "Fixin's," *Carolina Folk-Plays*, Second Series, edited by Frederick H. Koch (Henry Holt and Company, New York, 1924).

CHAPTER VII

1. Patricia McMullan, "Cottie Mourns," *American Folk Plays*, edited by Frederick H. Koch (D. Appleton–Century Company, New York, 1939).

2. Josephina Niggli, "Soldadera," *Mexican Folk Plays* (University of North Carolina Press, Chapel Hill, 1938).

3. Philip Parker, "Ancient Heritage," *American Folk Plays*, edited by Frederick H. Koch (D. Appleton–Century Company, New York, 1939).

4. Eugene O'Neill, *The Hairy Ape*. Copyright 1922 by Eugene O'Neill. Reprinted by courtesy of Random House, Inc., New York.

CHAPTER VIII

1. Paul Green, *The Lost Colony: An Outdoor Play in Two Acts* (University of North Carolina Press, Chapel Hill, 1937). (The play is produced annually on Roanoke Island, North Carolina, by the Roanoke Island Historical Association, under the management of D. Bradford Fearing.)

CHAPTER IX

1. Alexis Carrel, *Man the Unknown* (Harper & Brothers, New York, 1935), p. 144.

2. George W. Hartmann, *Gestalt Psychology* (The Ronald Press Company, New York, 1935), Chapter 8.

3. Albert R. Chandler, *Beauty and Human Nature* (D. Appleton–Century Company, New York, 1934), p. 212.

4. Joseph Hudnut, *Modern Sculpture* (W. W. Norton & Company, New York, 1929), p. 9.

5. Henry P. Bowie, *On the Laws of Japanese Painting* (Paul Elder & Company, San Francisco, 1911), pp. 35, 36, 77–78.

6. John Martin, *America Dancing* (Dodge Publishing Company, New York, 1936), p. 122.

BOOKS USEFUL TO
THE ACTOR AND DIRECTOR

(Works listed in the preceding references are not repeated here.)

Alberti, Madame Eva, *A Handbook of Acting Based on the New Pantomime* (Samuel French, New York, 1932).

Avery, Elizabeth, Dorsey, Jane, and Sickels, Vera A., *First Principles of Speech Training* (D. Appleton–Century Company, New York, 1929).

Barber, Philip W., *The Scene Technician's Handbook* (Whitlock's Book Store, New Haven, 1928).

Barton, Lucy, *Historic Costume for the Stage* (Walter H. Baker, Boston, 1935).

Boleslavsky, Richard, *Acting: The First Six Lessons* (Theatre Arts, New York, 1933).

Bosworth, Halliam, *Technique in Dramatic Art,* revised edition (The Macmillan Company, New York, 1934).

Brown, Gilmor, and Garwood, Alice, *General Principles of Play Direction* (Samuel French, New York, 1936).

Burris-Meyer, Harold, and Cole, Edward C., *Scenery for the Theatre* (Little, Brown & Company, Boston, 1938).

Calvert, Louis, *Problems of the Actor* (Henry Holt and Company, New York, 1918).

Cheney, Sheldon, *A World History of the Arts* (The Viking Press, New York, 1937).

Craig, Gordon, *On the Art of the Theatre* (Dodd, Mead and Company, New York, 1925).

Dean, Alexander, *Little Theatre Organization and Management* (D. Appleton–Century Company, New York, 1926).

Dolman, John, *The Art of Play Production* (Harper & Brothers, New York, 1928).

Dow, Arthur Wesley, *Composition*, revised edition (Doubleday, Doran and Company, New York, 1924).

Eustis, Morton, *Players at Work* (Theatre Arts, New York, 1937).

Factor, Max, *Hints on the Art of Make-up* (Max Factor Make-up Studios, Hollywood, 1936).

Fuchs, Theodore, *Stage Lighting* (Little, Brown & Company, Boston, 1929).

Fuerst, Walter René, and Hume, Samuel James, *Twentieth Century Stage Decoration* (Alfred A. Knopf, New York, 1929).

Gilder, Rosamond, *A Theatre Library: A Bibliography of One Hundred Books Relating to the Theatre* (Theatre Arts, New York, 1932).

Halstead, William Perdue, *Stage Management for the Amateur Theatre* (F. S. Crofts & Co., New York, 1937).

Heffner, Hubert C., Selden, Samuel, and Sellman, Hunton D., *Modern Theatre Practice*, second edition (F. S. Crofts & Co., New York, 1939).

Hinsdell, Oliver, *Making the Little Theatre Pay* (Samuel French, New York, 1925).

Hollingworth, H. L., *The Psychology of the Audience* (American Book Company, New York, 1935).

Holmes, F. Lincoln D., *A Handbook of Voice and Diction* (F. S. Crofts & Co., New York, 1940).

Hopkins, Arthur, *How's Your Second Act?* (Samuel French, New York, 1931).

Isaacs, Edith J. R., *Theatre* (Little, Brown & Company, Boston, 1927).

Jacobs, Lewis, *The Rise of the American Film* (Harcourt, Brace and Company, New York, 1939).

Jones, Robert Edmond, *Drawings for the Theatre* (Theatre Arts, New York, 1925).

Kempf, Dr. Edward J., *The Autonomic Functions and the Personality*, Nervous and Mental Disease Monograph No. 28 (Nervous and Mental Disease Publishing Company, New York, 1921).

Luckiesh, Matthew, *Color and Its Application*, second edition (D. Van Nostrand Company, New York, 1921).

Luckiesh, Matthew, *Light and Shade and Their Applications* (D. Van Nostrand Company, New York, 1916).

Martin, John, *Introduction to the Dance* (W. W. Norton & Company, New York, 1939).

McCandless, Stanley R., *A Method of Lighting the Stage* (Theatre Arts, New York, 1932).

Macgowan, Kenneth, *Footlights Across America* (Harcourt, Brace and Company, New York, 1929).

Macgowan, Kenneth, *The Theatre of Tomorrow* (Boni and Liveright, New York, 1921).

Naumberg, Nancy (editor), *We Make the Movies* (W. W. Norton & Company, New York, 1937).

Selden, Samuel, *A Player's Handbook* (F. S. Crofts & Co., New York, 1934).

Selden, Samuel, and Sellman, Hunton D., *Stage Scenery and Lighting: A Handbook for Nonprofessionals* (F. S. Crofts & Co., New York, 1930).

Simonson, Lee, *The Stage Is Set* (Harcourt, Brace and Company, New York, 1932).

Stanislavsky, Constantin, *An Actor Prepares*, translated by Elizabeth Reynolds Hapgood (Theatre Arts, New York, 1936).

Stanislavsky, Constantin, *My Life in Art* (Little, Brown & Company, Boston, 1927).

Stanton, Sanford E., *Theatre Management* (D. Appleton–
Century Company, New York, 1929).

Strauss, Ivard, *Paint, Powder and Make-up* (Sweet and Son,
New Haven, 1936).

Walkup, Fairfax P., *Dressing the Part* (F. S. Crofts & Co.,
New York, 1938).

INDEX